Talent Assessment

Talent Assessment

A New Strategy for Talent Management

TONY DAVIS WITH MAGGIE CUTT,
NEIL FLYNN, PETER MOWL and
SIMON ORME

Routledge
Taylor & Francis Group

LONDON AND NEW YORK

First published in paperback 2024

First published 2007 by Gower Publishing

Published 2016 by Routledge
4 Park Square, Milton Park, Abingdon, Oxon OX14 4RN

and by Routledge
605 Third Avenue, New York, NY 10158

Routledge is an imprint of the Taylor & Francis Group, an informa business

Copyright © 2007, 2016, 2024 Tony Davis

Publisher's Note
The publisher has gone to great lengths to ensure the quality of this reprint but points out that some imperfections in the original copies may be apparent.

British Library Cataloguing in Publication Data
Talent assessment : a new strategy for talent management
1. Personnel management 2. Human capital 3. Creative
ability in business 4. Strategic planning
I. Orme, Simon

Library of Congress Cataloging-in-Publication Data
Talent assessment : a new strategy for talent management / edited by Simon Orme ... [et al].
   p. cm.
   Includes index.
   ISBN: 978-0-566-08731-8
   1. Personnel management. 2. Ability. 3. Organizational effectiveness. I. Orme, Simon.
   HF5549.T194 2007
   658.3'14--dc22

                                                                        2006032962

ISBN 13: 978-0-566-08731-8 (hbk)
ISBN 13: 978-1-03-283788-8 (pbk)
ISBN 13: 978-1-315-61181-5 (ebk)

DOI: 10.4324/9781315611815

Contents

List of Figures

Acknowledgements

We would like to thank Alan Newman for all his help in identifying key issues in psychometric testing and also Lucy Scott and Andrew Davis for their assistance with the structure of the book and some of the design concepts.

Preface

Many companies have been involved with the concept of talent management in various forms for many years but without perhaps giving the concept the correct label. After all, nearly all companies have endeavoured to develop its best people through higher management potential programmes or some other means of fast-tracking the top performers. Experience has shown that the 20/80 rule that is applied to so many aspects of business does in the most part apply to the process of talent management. In other words, 80 per cent of a company's results can be attributed to 20 per cent of its employees. There is nothing particularly new in this but it is important to remember that potential top performers need to be selected with great care, thoroughly assessed and trained in accordance with a carefully planned programme with highly demanding requirements for outstanding results. While all this is going on, they need to be motivated, shown that the level of effort required will produce the size of reward promised, and then they need to be appraised very carefully: their motivation and creativity needs to be sustained at a very high level in a consistent manner.

Various reports have shown that very few people in an organization would strongly agree that their companies did an effective job in developing people to the right level. They would, however, support the fact that most companies were quite effective at dealing with people whose performance was below the standards expected.

These issues require careful consideration in order for corporate performance to be improved. The time has come where the best of talent management cannot simply be delegated to just some form of HR function on its own. It also has to involve senior line and staff management right up to CEO level, depending on the structure of the organization and its corporate goals.

In order to drive a talent management programme properly, one of the key factors is thorough performance appraisal. One could go so far as to say that the days of simple feedback between managers and subordinates are, if not over, very limiting and hardly likely to produce the right results. True talent needs to be isolated from its latent state by everybody who is likely to be affected by the capability of the individual concerned. In practice, this means that a number of external influences, in addition to the role of the immediate superior, has to be considered very carefully. This will be covered in Chapter 4 of this book in more detail but should be recognized as one of the key functions of ensuring that the essence of talent management is correctly addressed.

The way in which this book is structured is to examine each of the most important aspects of talent management, from the concept itself and why it is needed through various methods of assessment, appraisal, training and development and the use of information technology to support the corporate plan, followed by a self-assessment questionnaire designed to highlight the level of the reader's knowledge of talent management. Answers to the questionnaire are provided which will enable the reader, together with guidelines for interpreting the scores, to take a snapshot of their knowledge of the subject. Whether the reader is a senior line manager, a functional staff manager, a consultant or external contractor, this whole subject needs to be understood because of the integrated nature of effective talent management today and in the future.

A great deal of emphasis – in our opinion, correctly – has been placed upon the assessment of people to ensure that the right person is assigned the right job at the right time, to ensure that the risk of making the wrong hiring decision, or promoting the wrong person, is minimized and, hopefully eliminated, by thorough assessment procedures.

It is a known fact that hiring someone who subsequently turns out to be a recruitment error can be a very costly exercise. In the case of a salesperson, it is not just the salary and recruitment fee that is irrecoverable but the lost opportunity cost i.e. no return on the investment made in the assigned sales territory that causes the real loss, and that account for a substantial percentage of the cost of failure.

So what can we learn from these traditional recruitment failures? We need to aim for talent. We will clearly not always achieve our objectives in recruiting and developing a perfect team, but lowering recruitment standards just to provide people who can 'do the job' will inevitably result in a core of personnel who will perpetuate mediocrity. This is something no company needs and must be avoided as much as possible.

Of course, no organization can just hire pure talent that, having been assessed, will grow and adapt to the changing needs of the business indefinitely without proper monitoring. But if the recruitment standards are set at a very high but nevertheless achievable level and continuously reviewed, using the most rigorous methods of measurement, then surely we can raise the effectiveness of key contributors to support a thriving and developing business for many years to come. Not only that, we can do our best to recognize latent talent for new opportunities within the existing talent base.

Perhaps the most meaningful message that I have ever heard about a really talented high-flyer was made by her manager – 'Katie never, ever fails to amaze me, even at the earliest stage of a new assignment in which she is involved'.

Tony Davis

Foreword

For the last decade and a half, I have been involved in implementing some of the most significant developments in information technology through the various generations of hardware and software that have made large and small companies so much more effective in meeting their customers' needs, and in delivering sustained business performance.

Outstanding progress has been made in technology, yet the real roots of the service and performance revolution lie in the people who have created and delivered it. The IT industry talks loosely of technical drivers – yet who has ever seen technology drive anything? *Technology enables, people drive.*

At their heart, our organizations still and will remain people-driven – people with the right competencies, skills and experience for our particular businesses. Without the quality and commitment of our people, we cannot go far in pursuing, achieving and maintaining excellence.

This book has been written by a consortium of experts in the fields associated with what we now recognize as talent management – with the view of helping managers to recruit, develop and retain world-class winning teams – true talent, not just good practitioner performance.

Talent management is not just an extension or branch of the HR discipline. In today's world it is a very necessary board-led company discipline and capability, requiring managers specifically trained, appointed and assigned to ensure that the future of their businesses are in the best hands.

By selecting, developing and *retaining* demonstrably talented people, a company will save vast amounts of money and deliver the benefits of sustained performance improvement. A prime objective of talent management is to keep – and keep motivated – the best performers.

This motivation requires involving key people in realistic objective-setting, ensuring that they are aware of recognition programmes where effort and rewards are clearly defined, promoting a culture of continual learning and professional development – and stimulating their creativity! Above all they need to know that they are valued and listened to. They have no need to 'look elsewhere' for a better job.

This book provides positive, practical guidelines to encourage companies who are considering talent management to implement a suitable programme. It also introduces more advanced aspects of the subject, particularly in terms of assessing suitable candidates for this way of our future.

Dr Richard Sykes
Chairman, The Outsourcing & Offshore Group, Intellect
Former Group Vice President IT, ICI plc

CHAPTER 1

The Concept of Talent Management

INTRODUCTION

Talent management as a strategic management issue is a relatively new concept. Like quality management and time management, the titles provide some guidance to the meaning but, like quality and time, talent is an abstract concept that requires some definition.

We all have a general understanding of what talent is and probably share a belief that it is a desirable and valuable quality. Defining it is a different matter. A dictionary definition tells us that talent is 'a special aptitude or faculty' or 'a high mental ability'.

We frequently couple the quality with an activity and so we talk about a 'talented musician' or a 'talented footballer'. In both examples we imply a special aptitude or level of competence on the part of the individual. But what is talent management?

In the absence of a dictionary definition we have created our own:

'Talent management is the recruitment, development and retention of individuals who consistently deliver superior performance.'

This definition provides some guidance as to what is involved in implementing a talent management strategy and so acts as a broad reference point for the contents of this book.

A talent management strategy is a deliberate and structured corporate approach to the recruitment, retention and development of talented individuals within the organization. The intention is to employ people who will consistently deliver superior performance.

This is not an intellectual concept. High achievers make a disproportionate contribution to the prosperity of the enterprise and are a valuable commodity.

Talent is not restricted to particular grades or areas of responsibility. It appears at all work levels and in all functions. Like quality, we know it when we see it and are glad when we find it.

Management is the art of achieving results through the direction of people and activities. It is made much more effective if management itself is talented and if the people who are being managed have a talent for the work they are involved in.

On reflection, a talent management strategy is a 'no brainer'. We all know that talented people will produce superior results. Making it happen is a different consideration. Finding, deploying and managing them presents a number of challenges that in themselves require talent on the part of the executive team. Neither can we ignore the fact that talent presents a challenge. Able people are inclined to ask difficult questions and set a provocative agenda. This introduces dimensions of executive stress that many management teams prefer to avoid.

Talent management is a strategic issue. It is not a 'nice to have' or a 'coincidental benefit'. It is something that has to be worked for, planned and given executive attention. For those organizations that have made a conscious effort to address this issue, the rewards have proved to be outstanding. For those who have trusted to luck and hoped that their recruitment, development and management processes will somehow produce a talented workforce, the outcomes are at best problematical.

So what are the results of taking on talent management as a strategic issue? The initial benefits will be in terms of having a workforce which is inherently capable of doing a good job. This in itself is a valuable outcome. The fact that many of them will be capable of taking on wider responsibilities and be able to perform them well is a second benefit.

The third advantage is that senior appointments can be made from internal resources. This reduces the impact of disruption caused by the introduction of externally resourced appointments.

While the introduction of 'new blood' has its merits, it does have the disadvantage of giving a steep learning curve on the part of the new appointee and signalling to the existing workforce that they are 'not quite good enough' with a consequent impact upon morale and motivation.

How much better to have a strategy which seeks to recruit, develop and nurture internal talent that is capable of reaching the highest levels in the organization. This is what talent management is all about.

ELEMENTS OF TALENT MANAGEMENT

Our definition of talent management as being 'the recruitment, development and retention of individuals who consistently deliver superior performance' helps to identify the key elements of a talent management strategy.

In succeeding chapters we investigate some of these elements in detail, especially those which deal with psychometric testing and knowledge assessment. We also consider the roles of the HR function and the use of technology as an aid to performance management.

In our view, talent management should be treated as a holistic endeavour. Addressing individual elements has some merit but is unlikely to produce the same outcomes as a comprehensive approach.

From an operational perspective, there is always the need to find a balance between the investment and the return. Risk management is at the heart of all management strategies, if there is a guaranteed return for a specified investment then the risk element is largely eliminated. Unfortunately the majority of commercial decisions do not have that degree of certainty.

So where do the risks lie in implementing a talent management strategy?

For most executives, risks can be described under two headings – financial risk and political risk. The assumption being that the person taking the risk will be rewarded either financially or in terms of personal reputation – or possibly both.

FINANCIAL RISK

The financial risk is that the investment will not produce a positive or measurable return. The programmes and strategies advocated in this book do require some investment. The majority of the investment can be quantified but how should it be justified?

Chapter 2 seeks to identify where the benefits will manifest themselves. However, it is not possible to develop a precise 'return on investment' formula because many of the benefits are unquantifiable. To some extent the decision to adopt a talent management strategy is an act of faith. There are, of course, sectors where talent management has a direct bearing on the balance sheet, such as American and UK football clubs where the players are shown as multi-million dollar assets.

Acts of faith can generally be supported by an examination of the consequences of not adopting them, for example a talent management strategy. 'Why not?' is an argument that has been advanced by evangelists from time immemorial. The counter argument is equally timeworn: 'why?'. The next chapter explores this issue and seeks to identify the benefits propositions and value bases.

POLITICAL RISK

The political risk is that the proposed investment and strategy will not produce the proposed benefits and that those responsible for advocating them will be penalized. This is a very understandable consideration and is at the heart of many executive decisions.

Being 'right' or lucky' in decision-making is the hallmark of the successful executive; the converse also applies. The desire to mitigate risk is not necessarily a negative consideration – purely a human one. We all take risks in our daily lives and are familiar with precautionary strategies – crossing a busy road is inherently risky but we can reduce the possibility of an accident by a careful evaluation of traffic density, road width, visibility and our personal agility. If we want to totally avoid risk we could even find a bridge or secure crossing point – but that might take time and delay our progress.

So risk has another dimension – time.

The risk is that if an action is not taken at the right time the consequences of inaction will be dire. In evaluating the merits of adopting a talent management strategy, the consequences of inaction must be taken into account.

THE TIME IS NOW

The majority of new management thinking emanates from the United States. There are many reasons for this, not the least being the size of the domestic market which stimulates thinking on a grand scale. Early management thinking focused on manufacturing productivity; this was followed by logistics and distribution. The need to communicate with a large and diverse market led to the development of advertising and marketing strategies.

In more recent times much attention has been given to overall corporate performance and the relationship between the supplier and the customer. 'Just-in-time', lean manufacturing and 6Sigma are examples of this approach.

The latest focus is upon 'human capital' – the skills and competencies of the employees and ways in which they are deployed, managed and exploited. This concept has gained rapid acceptance and the existence of relevant strategies is now expected as part of any corporate governance assessment.

The recognition of the merits of human capital management is spreading, as witnessed by the great expansion in the number of papers presented at conferences on the subject and the general level of discussion that it is attracting. Talent management has arrived and justifies its place in the executive portfolio.

SOURCING TALENT

Sourcing talented people is one of the key elements of a talent management strategy. The others are talent retention and development.

What we are looking for is a talent pool, a group of identified individuals which can be developed over a period of time and treated as a specific investment. The key issues are how do we source them and where do they come from?

Talent can be sourced from two different pools – external and internal. Any structured talent management strategy will need to consider both sources but my preference would always be to begin with an internal trawl. Existing employees have a number of advantages, not the least being their knowledge of the organization and the knowledge that the organization has of them.

In either case, the search for talent can only begin once the selection criteria have been identified. Therefore the starting point is the development of a talent filter which can be used to evaluate potential candidates.

In the past I have been exposed to a number of selection techniques which have ranged from the exotic to the banal. However, those which have impressed me have included elements which are included in the following Talent Search Matrix.

TALENT SEARCH MATRIX

The thinking behind the Talent Search Matrix is to combine a number of quantifiable and unquantifiable elements which, when taken together, paint a picture of an individual who is likely to produce the desired results. The important thing is to focus on the qualities that are required rather than to produce a job description.

There are six elements in the matrix:

- experience, Profile, Qualification; and

- expertise, Potential, Quantification.

Experience, profile and qualification can all be subjected to objective assessments, while expertise, potential and quantification depend more upon the subjective dimension.

These six elements are used to create the candidate description and are described in the following sections. Another dimension is that the first three elements reflect past and present characteristics whilst the second set are all related to future performance.

EXPERIENCE

This is a description of the experiences that the candidate will have been exposed to. It could include periods in line or staff functions, responsibility for team leadership, budget and goal setting, staff training and project management.

PROFILE

This may be determined by psychometric testing or personality profiling. The description under this heading will identify desirable traits such as creativity, ability to work under pressure, judgement, ambition and energy levels.

QUALIFICATION

This description will identify desirable levels of academic achievement or professional qualifications. It could also look for other qualifications including relevant training, language skills or international experience.

EXPERTISE

This will identify particular personal strengths and knowledge sets that are required. Desirable qualities might include the ability to handle change, technical literacy, communication skills and intellectual flexibility.

POTENTIAL

This will identify the ultimate level of responsibility that the selected candidates should be able to aspire to. Not all members of the talent pool are potential chief executives but they should all be capable of filling senior executive positions.

QUANTIFICATION

These are the levels of achievement that candidates should be capable of in operational terms. They could include the ability to integrate an acquisition, effect a profit turnaround, manage an overseas branch or launch a new product.

The completion of the characteristics sought under each of these headings is no easy task but the proper execution of this exercise will be a valuable aid in setting out the parameters of the search. We have found this to be a useful topic at planning meetings as it forces the management team to really question assumptions about current competencies and future potential.

EXTERNAL SOURCING

Adding to the talent pool through external sourcing would always be our second choice. We would only embark on this route once we were satisfied that we did not have the necessary pool of talent available from internal resources.

However, if this proves to be the case then we would use the Talent Search Matrix as the basis for the recruiting programme.

DEVELOPING TALENT

THE CASE FOR TALENT DEVELOPMENT

The interview process is unlikely to produce the finished article. This means that some attention must be devoted to developing a range of skills and characteristics which will enable individual potential to be achieved.

Some of the desired talent matrix elements will be inherent in the individual, whilst others will be acquired either formally or informally. The talent development strategy should therefore contain the following elements:

- assessment: of competencies, capabilities and potential
- training needs analysis: identification of talent matrix deficiencies
- training programme: provision of education and training programmes
- impact assessment: measurement of the impact of the training programme.

The strategy is designed to produce individuals who have the competence and capability to produce superior results on a consistent basis.

SKILLS AND KNOWLEDGE DEVELOPMENT

Part of the development strategy will be devoted to equipping the individual with the knowledge and skills required to perform the allocated role or function.

Some of this training will focus upon professional and technical skills employed in the function role, for example selling, project management or logistics. Other formal training will be related to specific corporate processes or techniques such as manufacturing processes, delivery channels or purchasing and procurement.

The overall objective is to equip the individual with the necessary skills and knowledge to be able to perform the function.

As the individual progresses through the organization, so the levels and bodies of knowledge will expand. One key consideration is the extent to which the training programme is designed to prepare the individual for the next role and responsibility.

Too often there is an assumption that an outstanding individual in one role can be slotted into a higher role without any preparation. A classic example is a high achieving salesperson who is promoted to sales management without any training in the techniques and responsibilities of the new role. The natural consequence is that the individual flounders in the changed environment, loses confidence and has to be either rescued or relieved.

DEVELOPING PERSONAL SKILLS

Our talent-pool candidates are identified as having the potential to rise to senior executive or chief executive roles. In order to achieve their potential they will have to demonstrate their capabilities in a number of line and functional roles as they progress towards the ultimate goal. Along this progression they will acquire and develop technical and professional competencies but they will also need to develop a number of personal characteristics which will be needed in their ultimate role.

The profiles of senior and chief executives in terms of personal traits and characteristics are the subject of numerous management text books. Desirable qualities include leadership, insight, focus, dedication, integrity, communication skills, numeracy and literacy, and ambition.

This list is not exhaustive but it does indicate that something rather more than technical and professional competence is required. The question is whether these are inherent qualities or whether they can be acquired either formally or through some form of osmosis.

FORMAL AND INFORMAL TRAINING

Some elements of the development strategy will be delivered through formal training and education programmes. Others will be delivered through informal education generally supplied through coaching and mentoring arrangements.

We think it is important to note the difference between the roles of coaches and mentors. Coaches show people how to do things, while mentors fill the role of trusted advisers. A typical coach would be an experienced manager in the department who helps a newly appointed manager to understand how to perform in the new role.

A mentor is typically a senior executive who acts as a guide on corporate procedures and, of necessary, internal politics. The mentor is also a reference point against which the mentored person can test ideas, assumptions and possibilities.

It is from the relationships with coaches and mentors that the individual begins to develop the characteristics and insights that will be needed in senior roles.

TRAINING IMPACT ANALYSIS

Training and education programmes have as their objectives the transfer of skills, knowledge and changes in behaviour. They can represent significant areas of expenditure, and the time involved on the part of those being trained can have an impact on business performance.

It seems sensible, then, to have some means of measuring the effectiveness of the various forms of training that are being invested in. This is the objective of training impact analysis.

At the simplest level this involves a three-stage process:

1.   assessment of competence levels prior to training;

2.   conduct of the training event;

3.   assessment of the new level of competence after training.

Such an approach will serve two purposes. It will measure the impact on the individual and also, over a period of time, measure the effectiveness of the training methods used.

MANIFESTATIONS OF TALENT

In any organization a number of people will stand out as having something rather special about them. This differentiation is generally based upon a combination of personality and performance.

At first glance these individuals may appear to be natural members of the talent pool, but we believe that it is important to apply some further tests in order to validate their apparent claims for selection.

From our experience and observation, truly talented people demonstrate a number of key characteristics which are identifiable under a number of headings.

CAPABILITY IN THE ROLE

This is the ability to deliver superior results in any allocated role. This is an important distinction and separates those who are specialists from the wider competence of the generalists. We have observed that those who are able to perform well in any role adopt a structured approach to any new challenge. This involves the following process:

- assess the nature of the challenge;

- identify the key performance metrics;

- determine how to achieve them;

- implement the execution plan.

In executing this plan they will not be afraid to ask for help and guidance from experienced practitioners. Neither will they be slow to seek training to equip them with the skills needed to deliver superior performance in the role.

ABILITY TO HANDLE CHANGE

Change is an inherent element of corporate life. Change is either imposed by external forces such as regulations or legislation, or self-induced in order to react to market forces or to exploit emerging opportunities.

In both instances the organization will need to adapt to change and implement necessary alterations to structures, processes and procedures. These changes will be implemented by management and staff and can have a disruptive effect.

The ability to embrace change as a necessary part of corporate evolution is a desirable characteristic and one shared by talented people. The able person will recognize that change is not a disruption to an organized life, but is the source of a new challenge and a further opportunity to demonstrate competence and capabilities.

Talented people are not afraid of change and in their approach to a challenge will be prepared to consider different ways of achieving the desired outcomes.

CAPACITY FOR LEARNING

For the able person the ability to master new skills is an essential part of personal development. Talented people are inherently curious and seek to expand their knowledge and skills sets through formal and informal education.

They also demonstrate an intellectual capacity for the rapid absorption of new concepts and techniques, but equally have a questioning approach which is a filtering technique they use to extract the key elements of any new concept.

This capacity for learning is also demonstrated in their ability to manage change and rapidly adapt to altered environments.

PERSONAL PROFILE

Talented people seem to share a number of common personality characteristics. The most common one is a degree of self-confidence based upon their ability to master current and new challenges. This self-belief is based upon the techniques they have adopted to help them analyse tasks and develop effective processes to deliver superior performance.

They also demonstrate good communication skills in both the written and spoken word. This verbal acuity is a necessary element in gaining acceptance of their ideas and operational processes and through them the achievement of their objectives.

This combination of confidence and communication ability is frequently accompanied by a reasoning ability which allows them to apply a disciplined approach to problem-solving. The ability to analyse facts in a dispassionate manner and construct acceptable and practical solutions is a valuable characteristic.

A final common characteristic is focus. This is the ability to concentrate on the key elements for performance success and not allowing other events or factors to distract them from their primary goal. This can sometimes make them appear to be impersonal or results oriented, but this is because their motivations are not aligned to pursuing popularity. They are confident that their achievements will speak for themselves.

BURN-OUT AND PEAKING

PLATEAU POTENTIAL

Not every employee with latent potential will achieve their ultimate goal. The very nature of the pyramid structure of most organizations ensures that only a small part of the population will reach the highest roles.

As a consequence, some members of the talent pool will plateau out at some point in their careers. Managing the arrival of the plateau and then managing the consequences of it for the individual is an executive challenge.

The plateau is arrived at when it is determined that the individual does not have the required skills to advance to the next rank or to perform adequately in it. This point can be reached for a number of reasons:

- diminution of performance in the current role;

- not eligible for promotion to the next rank;

- overtaken by a rising star and so blocked for further promotion;

- inwilling or unable to accept the conditions of the next appointment.

None of these causes necessarily means that the individual has ceased to be a valuable employee. They merely signify that further promotion is unlikely.

MANAGING FAILURE

Progress to the top is unlikely to be accomplished without some dips in performance during the upwards progression.

One of the tests of the capabilities of an individual is how they manage failure. Failure can take a variety of forms and have varying degrees of severity. Some people are destroyed by apparent or real failure to achieve their objectives. Others benefit from the experience and emerge as better and stronger individuals as a result of the experience.

Where performance falls below the targets set, it is important to identify the cause. In some instances the target itself may have been unachievable or external forces may have made it an impossible goal.

Where there were defects in process or planning, it is necessary to identify what they were and how such an outcome can be avoided in the future.

Similarly, where sub-performance is delivered, it is necessary to identify whether the causes were a lack of skill or functional knowledge. If either of these were the cause, then appropriate training programmes will be required in order to remedy the defects.

Public failure to achieve set objectives will hit hard on an able individual. It is important to recognize the potential impact upon personal confidence and esteem, and to help the individual to recover and use the experience as part of the learning curve. Really able people will be able to do this and will have learned some valuable lessons from the experience.

HORIZONTAL DEVELOPMENT

Many organizations plan individual careers on the basis of a mix of line and staff functions. The objective is to broaden their horizons and expose them to a variety of corporate responsibilities.

Most senior responsibilities involve a mix of staff and line functions anyway and so this approach is a useful way of developing competence in both aspects of corporate work. There is also an increasing tendency in international companies of giving high fliers overseas experience so that they develop a global perspective.

A further trend is moving people between line departmental roles. Periods in sales, manufacturing, logistics or customer service will all help to develop a wider corporate perspective.

The existence of a structured horizontal development strategy also provides an opportunity to find a new role for an individual who has not delivered the expected results in their current role.

UP OR OUT

There is a general assumption that a talented individual will progress through the organization through a series of upward promotions. This progress may be delayed if there is a dip in performance, in which case there may be a recovery period in another role where the individual is given a chance to rebuild career momentum.

When this does not happen, there is the question of how to handle the situation. In some corporate cultures the pressure for continuous upward progression is so strong that any dip in performance is a signal for career out or expulsion from the talent pool (which can have the same effect).

Whilst we have a high regard for the pursuit of superior performance as a corporate ethos, it does seem to be that the termination of previously high fliers who have reached their plateau of achievement is an expensive indulgence. Good people who have peaked are still good people and should be found roles where they can play to their strengths and still make a positive contribution to the organization.

Such individuals will need careful coaching and mentoring in their new status and may even get a second wind. As a general policy, we think it is a necessary part of any talent management strategy to make provision for those who may fall by the wayside.

RETAINING AND REWARDING TALENT

TALENT RETENTION

Recruiting, developing and retaining talented people are the objectives of a talent management strategy. Retaining them within the organization while they develop is therefore a key issue. An organization which is known for the excellence of its staff becomes a target for the attentions of the executive search fraternity.

Some companies, at various points in their history, have acquired such a high profile for the quality of their functional competence that they have become standard setters in their sectors. Procter and Gamble for marketing, Ford for finance, IBM for selling and Marks & Spencer for merchandising come to mind as exemplars of best practice at various points in the last two decades.

What was interesting about these particular companies was that, when they were at their zenith, they were notoriously difficult to recruit from. They had somehow managed to achieve that ideal position where their top performers could leave to join any other company but chose not to.

There are, of course, many other companies where similar conditions existed. The key people knew individually and collectively who were the winners and that the sense of excitement and sense of achievement were at such a high level that they were, in many cases, immune to approaches from other organizations.

One particular company stands out as a classic example of this culture. In the early 1970s an IT professional had joined a major software house as a senior consultant. Three years later he was offered the role of Managing Director by a small Canadian company. The opportunity was too good to miss and so he took it. Colleagues at the software house tried to dissuade him from leaving but, when they saw that he was determined to leave, they agreed that it was a good opportunity and wished him well. Not only that but, when he had settled into the new role, he kept in touch and his ex-Managing Director acted as a remote mentor.

Nine years and two periods as Managing Director later, he was approached by a number of companies, one of which was the original software house. He had no hesitation about rejoining and spent a further ten years with them. A number of their colleagues were similar returnees which spoke volumes for the culture developed by the founder, which encouraged every employee to develop their careers to their maximum potential even if it meant leaving the company.

CAREER INVESTMENT

As we have seen, one of the elements of a talent management company is development. The employing company needs to demonstrate that it is prepared to make investments in its staff in order to help them acquire additional skills and knowledge as their careers develop. Employers want their staff to invest their careers in the company but need to show that this will be reciprocated by a similar investment in career development.

Where this implicit contract is sustained and executed, both sides to the contract will prosper and a virtuous circle is created in which talented people want to join (and stay), and the organization, as a result of superior performance, is able to make the necessary investments.

The corporate investment is not just in the provision of training. It includes the quality of the recruitment process, internal communication, HR infrastructure and the entire talent management strategy. Where all of these elements are in place, the company becomes an 'employer of choice' which in itself becomes a valuable element in attracting and retaining talented resources.

CORPORATE LOYALTY

Corporate loyalty is earned, not bought. High salaries and extensive benefits will not buy loyalty. In fact, unless superior corporate performance is achieved, and this means employing talented people, above-market salary levels cannot be sustained.

Many high performing companies do not pay premium salaries. People join and stay because of the perceived opportunities for career development and promotion prospects.

When key players who tell us that they want to leave because they have been offered a 'better job' have approached us, my first reaction is to ask them about the career prospects in the new company. Very often the 'better job' turns out to be more pay for an equivalent role. We would rarely support the offer of an increased salary to keep a key player and would always insist in discussing the future career prospects and making sure that the new role has at least equivalent potential. This does not always work but, more often than not, it does.

Building corporate loyalty comes from showing that the employer is prepared to match the investment made by the employee. Where the relationship is seen to be entirely one-sided and exploitative on the part of the employer, corporate loyalty will have little chance of developing.

As we said earlier, the target situation is where the employees are good enough to get a job anywhere else but choose to stay.

PROMOTION PROCESSES

A key element of any career development programme is the opportunity for promotion. For this to be an effective talent retention strategy, the promotion process must be open and transparent.

Nothing has a bigger impact upon employee commitment than the belief that their achievements are overlooked and that they have not been considered for promotion. Also, nothing destroys employee morale quicker than the belief that promotion is based upon personal relationships rather than on proven ability.

We firmly believe that candidates for promotion should be selected on the basis of having achieved selected performance targets and that the selection process is open, independent and public.

The establishment of a formal promotion panel or board, staffed by representatives from a number of corporate functions and managed by the HR function, will do much to build trust in the transparency of the activity.

A persistent problem in many organizations is the desire on the part of managers to keep high achievers in their teams. This can often have the effect of creating the impression that the only way to get promotion is to leave. An open and formal promotion assessment programme will prevent this happening to the advantage of both the employer and employee.

Most senior managers have sat on a number of promotion boards and have regularly made the point to candidates for promotion that a failure to pass the board assessment is not the end of their careers. Very often it is an opportunity to identify areas where improvement is sought and what needs to be achieved in order to be more successful next time. If this is done in a frank and open manner, then it will help to build trust in the fairness of the process.

COMPENSATION STRATEGIES

Should members of the talent pool be paid a salary premium? Our response would be no. Their rewards will come from opportunities for accelerated promotion by virtue of their superior performance. Depending upon their functional roles they may also be eligible for performance bonuses which, if they are superior performers, should be above the norm.

Talented people are rare and valuable assets, both internally and externally. In order to attract and retain them, the pay rates or salary bands at each level in the organization should reflect general market conditions.

One level of job satisfaction is comparative earning rates at specific ages. The ability to earn more than your contemporaries as a result of accelerated promotion is more satisfactory than being paid more for an equivalent role. Our experience with Business School students is that comparative earning rates at equivalent ages is a significant driver for performance.

DEVELOPING A TALENT MANAGEMENT STRATEGY

BACKGROUND THOUGHTS

In the previous section we have explored various aspects of talent management from an executive perspective. Our comments are based on direct practical experience and observation.

A very senior manager who spent most of his professional life in the computer services sector had, for a high proportion of that time, direct responsibility for profit and loss performance. The people with whom he worked were classic knowledge workers – intellectually able, highly motivated and ambitious. They operated in a highly competitive market and sold intangible services to sophisticated and challenging users.

This senior manager quickly realized the impact that really talented practitioners could have on the bottom line. The obvious conclusion was to seek to employ more of them and, most importantly, keep those that he had.

This is how he became involved in talent management although he did not realize it at the time.

He also had the privilege of working for some very talented senior executives. He observed their habits and sought to learn from them.

One conclusion is that talented people are not easy to manage. They are a demanding group and expect their manager to share their drive and defend their positions. Nearly all found the challenges associated with effective management of such people a stimulation, and knew that any decisions that were taken to optimise the management processes would need to stand the test of closer inspection.

One of the quiet satisfactions is seeing how many of the people identified as high achievers would go on to build really successful careers and, in a number of cases, run their own companies.

The case for developing a talent management strategy is unquestionable. As a chief executive one could not do without it and as an employer one would want to see evidence of it in any prospective employee.

SETTING THE STRATEGY

A talent management strategy is a strategic issue. It needs to be sponsored from the top of the organization and then enabled through a comprehensive infrastructure. A talent management strategy does not just happen as a result of an executive dictate. It has to be constructed on a progressive basis with buy-in at all levels.

A number of people have asked how to set about developing and implementing a talent management strategy. Here is a summary of some practical advice given to a Chief Executive:

BOARD INVOLVEMENT

There needs to be complete buy-in at the executive board level. To do this it would be necessary to prepare a short board paper covering the following issues:

1. What are we doing about recruiting, developing and retaining talented people in our company?

2. Can we identify the talented people in our company?

3.   What are we doing about succession planning?

4.   What management skills and resources will we need to achieve over a three-year plan?

5.   Is there any reason why we should not adopt a talent management strategy?

Hopefully the outcome from this discussion will lead to a general acceptance of the policy.

HR INVOLVEMENT

Having obtained general executive board agreement, the next question will be 'How do we do it?'

At this stage the HR team needs to be brought in and presented with the challenge of preparing an outline plan of how the strategy could be developed and implemented, together with any cost implications. In order to obtain expert assistance in the execution of the strategy it may be necessary to hire a talent management specialist; the associated costs should be included in the HR plan.

The talent management strategic plan should then be presented to the executive board and their approval obtained.

CORPORATE INVOLVEMENT

Once the plan has obtained approval, it is important to communicate the strategic intent within the organization. This communication should explain the objectives and also how and when the programme will be implemented.

The executive board should then be kept informed about the progress of the programme development and implementation.

PROGRAMME EXECUTION

Once the strategy has been implemented, it is important to ensure that it becomes part of the fabric and ethos of the organization and continues to have executive visibility.

Its existence will be a valuable asset in recruitment but can also be used to support the development of the corporate brand and in external marketing communications.

CASE STUDIES

CASE STUDY 1: AN ORGANIZATION STRUCTURE FOR TALENT MANAGEMENT

The situation

Many organizations introduce a talent management strategy by grafting it onto an existing organization structure. This case study describes an approach in which the talent management strategy was an integral part of the organization structure and was the basis on which it was developed.

The fundamental corporate philosophy was to make employees responsible for delivering real profits as soon as possible in their careers and then progressively giving them larger responsibilities as their capabilities developed. Embodied within this philosophy was a concept called a 'fully burdened profit centre'.

In this concept a profit centre bore its direct costs plus an allocated share of the corporate overheads. These costs, together with the revenues generated by the profit centre, were used to produce a real P&L position on a monthly basis. The cumulative results for the profit centres in the division produced a divisional P&L outcome and the cumulative divisional results produced the Group outcome.

Key issues

The key issues in this structural approach were as follows:

- The equitable allocation of overheads and indirect costs to the individual profit centres.

- The development of an effective reporting and forecasting system which would operate at the lowest reporting level and which would allow for progressive aggregation within the divisions and up to Group level.

- The recruitment, development and training of staff who were able to perform within this structure and thrive in this culture.

- The development of an effective annual planning process which was a combination of top-down and bottom-up parameters in which the business objectives of the profit centres were assimilated into the Group growth plans and objectives.

The ways in which some of these issues were dealt with are discussed in the following section.

Problems to overcome

The major challenge was the allocation of the overheads to be profit centres. At the Group level there were direct and indirect costs to be accumulated and allocated. The Group overheads included Finance and Premises administration, Group HR, Group Marketing, the Group Managing Director and the Divisional Managing Directors who each took responsibility for roughly half of the company. To these direct costs were added indirect costs, which included their shares of rent, heat, light, telephones, office equipment and so on, and any direct operating budgets.

The sum of these collective overheads was allocated to each of the operating divisions on the basis of their projected headcount for the forthcoming financial year.

This approach alone was one of the inherent strengths of the strategy because it encouraged the profit centre managers to review and challenge the growth and cost of the Group overhead functions. Their reward and recognition programme was based upon the achievement of target profits made after bearing their share of Group overheads.

The author of this case study was a senior executive of the company at this time and can attest to the very vigorous and frank discussions that occurred in the annual planning process when Group overheads were being compiled and allocated.

The Group Marketing Director had to justify the size of the team, their contribution and the returns that could be expected from the Group Marketing promotional budget. Similar questions were raised about the Group Finance and Group HR functions. This combination of checks and balances, together with the transparency of the process, was a part of the talent development programme. Ambitious profit centre managers, keen to demonstrate their ability to deliver superior profits, kept a watchful eye on any expenditure which did not make a measurable contribution to their bottom line or which compromised their ability to deliver their profit targets.

One external commentator described the company as being similar to a tramp steamer – 'it would go anywhere and do anything to make money and didn't carry any passengers'.

A second serious challenge was to find a balance between a 'robber baron' mentality and a 'good for the Group' ethos.

At the core of this challenge was another hidden aspect of the talent management strategy which was the acquisition and development of superior performers.

At the profit centre level a profit centre manager would want to attract and retain fee earners of high ability. A strong team spirit was encouraged and developed and, if the unit was having a good year, morale soared and an almost exclusive ethos developed.

While this was both desirable and welcomed, there were some negative side effects. One was the development of 'turf wars' in which different profit centres would compete for the same business, often to the confusion of the prospect or customer concerned, and frequently to the disadvantage of the Group.

In theory, one of the roles of the Divisional Managing Directors was to arbitrate between competing factions and to decide where the geographical territory boundaries lay. A classic problem was a situation where a prospect or customer with a headquarters in one territory but an operating unit in another: the issue was which territory owned the account.

A second side effect was the development of a 'silo' attitude in which the resources in a profit centre were regarded as being the exclusive property of that unit. A problem arose when one unit had temporary spare capacity while another was severely overstretched. While this was to be expected as part of normal business cycles, it was not contributory to the optimization of overall Group performance if there was no provision for resource sharing. This was facilitated through the use of a cross-charging process that was in effect an internal market under which spare capacity on one profit centre could be sold, at cost plus a small margin, to another, which had excessive demand.

These issues all became part of the fabric of the corporate culture, and their underlying concepts formed an important part of the induction process for new recruits. The profit focus ethos was an integral element in the organization structure and the organization structure reflected and supported it.

The key problem was the communication of the strategy as an operating philosophy. This was achieved through a combination of structure, process and staff development.

The ways in which it was done are described in the next section.

The solution

The growth of the company depended upon the recruitment, development and retention of able professionals who were able to thrive in a challenging and highly competitive environment.

A graduate intake programme was introduced in order to provide an annual injection of trainees with the desired intellectual capacity.

Their first year was a combination of technical training and field experience at the profit centres to which they were assigned. At the start of each year the individual profit centres would identify the number of graduate entries that they would require and they also bore their share of the recruitment and training costs.

The overall graduate entry programme was administered by the Group HR function, which also tracked the development of individual recruits in their early years. One of the objectives of this process was to attempt to identify patterns and trends which would help in ensuring that the initial selection process could identify the characteristics of those recruits which made the best progress in terms of career development.

For those within the company who had passed through the training programme, the career development process took them through a series of increasing levels of responsibility for achieving specific results.

This was an intrinsic talent management strategy that was reinforced by the corporate culture.

As individuals demonstrated their ability to operate at one level of responsibility – for example, team leadership or project management – they became eligible for roles with greater scope and responsibility.

They became thoroughly familiar with all of the management reporting and forecasting processes because on a monthly basis they were exposed to it and participated in it.

They also became familiar with financial planning and profit modelling because they were also a part of the annual budget planning process.

At certain stages in their careers they were brought to the attention of the promotion panel. One of the objectives of this panel was to ensure that high performers in one division were not overlooked as potential appointees for managerial or executive roles in other areas where vacancies had developed.

Outcome and benefits achieved

The application of this approach and structure created a company that delivered outstanding rates of growth and profit stability over an extended period.

The culture and ethos meant that the company was able to make rapid adjustments to market conditions and always had a strong team of young executives who were able to exploit new opportunities.

The company had management strength in depth and could quickly identify a rising star who could manage a new challenge. The quality and power of the underlying approach was reflected in the approach adopted by those who left to lead other companies in that they invariably implemented similar concepts in their new roles.

The culture also created a high degree of corporate loyalty as evidenced by the number of times executives left to develop and advance their careers and at a later stage were happy to return and bring their extended expertise with them.

Reinforcement programme

In the early days the corporate culture was absorbed by new recruits through a process of osmosis – they learnt through watching and copying. As the company expanded it was recognized that the processes needed formal documentation and training because the rate of expansion precluded the application of the osmosis practice.

A formal performance review and annual assessment programme was introduced for the same reasons and also to ensure consistency across the company.

The promotion panel was established with a formal process for nominating candidates for promotion. Copies of recent performance reviews supported these applications. At the senior levels specialized training courses were identified which provided education in corporate planning, programme management and a variety of soft skills.

Although there was no formal sponsored MBA programme, the company did regularly recruit senior managers with this qualification and absorbed their expertise into the culture.

Although the company had not set out to develop a formal talent management strategy, the structure it adopted and the corporate culture which surrounded it contributed to the development of a talent philosophy which contained all the characteristics of a formal strategy.

CHAPTER 2

Why is it Necessary? The Case for Talent Management

THE CASE FOR TALENT MANAGEMENT

INTRODUCTION

In Chapter 1 we looked at talent management as a concept and the various considerations that are involved in developing and implementing a talent management strategy. In this Chapter we will examine various aspects of the business case for adopting this approach.

Any business case will contain elements of cost, time and return and will expect to be able to identify a return on investment expressed in terms of payback and yield.

A talent management strategy is a corporate strategy. When implemented it will apply to all areas of the organization and there will be different manifestations of its impact in different functions, departments or units.

The measures of achievement in sales will be quite different from those in production, procurement or logistics. As a starting point it is useful to identify what is meant by performance excellence in each functional area of the organization and what the impact would be upon the overall performance of the organization if these levels could all be achieved and sustained.

SURVIVING OR ACHIEVING

Much of corporate life is determined by fixed time lines within the financial year. Daily, weekly or monthly performance reports lead to quarterly forecasts which are used to monitor achievement against the annual business plan. External and internal changes have to be accommodated in real time, as do major events such as product launches, the implementation of new computer systems or acquisition integration.

The pace of activity is unremitting in itself without the tyranny of the need to produce and present periodic reports on performance.

The pressure to manage activities within fixed time frames tends to develop a 'survival' mentality in which individuals are forced to take routes or adopt strategies that enable them to complete their workloads at a merely 'satisfactory' level.

One of the key objectives of a talent management strategy is to break the survival model and stimulate an achieving mentality. Performance is driven through practice, process and people. With the right people the implementation of practice (what we do), and process (how we do it) will deliver performance improvements. Talented people will also find ways to improve both practice and process in their pursuit of superior performance.

BUILDING WINNING TEAMS

Most organizations depend for their prosperity on the achievement of excellence in particular aspects of their activities. Their strengths can lie in sales, research, production or project execution.

Whilst there is a desire for generic performance excellence across all operating fronts it seems to me to be sensible to focus attention on key areas of strength as an initial tactic.

We would also have a look at those areas where there is the perceived greatest weakness with the objective of 'averaging up' overall performance.

Winning teams are built around winning people and so the ability to identify and develop talented team members is an absolute requirement.

In some organizations we have seen the development of 'hit squads'. These are small teams of high achievers who are assigned the trouble spots with the objective of securing both performance improvement in the short term and rebuilding the competence of the target operation. The establishment of such a team also provides a platform for the development of high achievers and allows them to extend their experience.

PLANNING FOR THE FUTURE

Much of corporate life is devoted to meeting daily challenges – the need to close a key deal, meet a delivery deadline or achieve a production target. It is necessary for there to be considerable focus on developing resources and individuals which can be used to manage current activities.

There is a danger that focus on present performance can overlook future requirements. There is much talk in management circles about 'business agility', the ability of organizations to adapt rapidly to a changing environment and exploit emerging opportunities.

While this is a logical approach which is supported by the numerous examples of companies which relied upon past performance and then foundered when they were overtaken by nimbler competitors, it can overlook the human dimensions of change.

Succession planning should look beyond the identification of candidates who can fill existing roles. It should take into account the roles that will need to be filled as a result of evolutionary or revolutionary corporate change.

The growth in outsourcing provides a classic example. The outsourcing of non-critical functions to a third party in order to obtain cost benefits or productivity gains is an established strategy but brings with it the need for special skills in managing the relationship and ensuring that the terms of the service level agreement are achieved. Relationship management is a new management skill and is a key element in ensuring that the benefits sought from the outsourcing agreement are obtained.

LEADING FROM THE FRONT

Talent management is a strategic issue and so warrants board attention. As such it requires sponsorship at board level plus continuing support from the HR function.

In some organizations the importance of the talent management strategy is signalled by the appointment of a specialist executive in the form of a Director of Talent Management or similar title. As talent management is a relatively new field, people with extensive experience are relatively scarce but the appointment of a specialist will do much to empower the programme.

The appointment of a formal promotion board with clear and transparent terms of reference will also help to build confidence in the application of the talent management strategy.

MANAGEMENT STYLE AND STRUCTURE

CORPORATE CULTURE

In order to deliver the potential benefits, the talent management strategy will have to co-exist with the prevailing corporate culture.

If the corporate culture is inimitable with the talent management strategy it will compromise the potential benefits. If this is the case, it may be necessary to change the corporate culture.

Corporate culture is as difficult to define as quality. It is more easily defined in terms of what it does than what it is. We are all familiar with the corporate statement that 'our people are our greatest asset' but those which have a 'people-supporting' culture do something about it.

Where a 'people-supporting' culture truly exists it will have a number of obvious manifestations, including the following:

- a structured recruitment process

- a formal skills development and training programme

- a formal promotion board

- a comprehensive annual performance review process

- a fully resourced HR function

- a genuine respect for the individual and a desire to develop individual potential.

Within the managerial levels there will be a strong focus on such dimensions as:

- team building and leadership

- staff development and training

- coaching and mentoring of staff

as well as measurements of functional performance and target achievement. The key point is that processes and practices exist that support the claim that the people assets are truly valued.

MANAGEMENT STYLE

A corporate style which is people-supporting at the corporate level needs to be delivered through a combination of executive focus and managerial style.

It is at the managerial interface that the practical application of the culture is delivered and where the impact is felt by individual employees. The achievement of this objective is not accomplished by executive dictat. It has to be built into the fabric of the organization.

Management training in the application of the corporate culture is a key requirement and their competence in executing this dimension of their functional responsibilities should be given a high profile in their annual performance assessment.

We believe that it is important to develop a management style which embraces a combination of hard and soft skills. The hard skills relate to the achievement of set goals and objectives, while soft skills have to do with people management and development.

ORGANIZATION STRUCTURE

The nature of the organization structure can have a direct impact upon the talent development strategy. There is an increasing trend towards the adoption of flat structures comprising multiple business and functional units with the objective of shortening the lines of communication and command.

A structure which allows individuals to take early responsibility for achieving specific results has much to commend it and provides a fertile training ground for future leaders.

In one organization, the corporate structure was based on a hierarchy of responsibilities starting with team leadership and progressing to project management and business unit management. The business unit managers had full profit and loss responsibility and were able to make decisions within their operating budgets on issues such as recruitment, marketing and product development.

In many respects they were chief executives of small businesses and as such created a team of potential future leaders.

The converse is the hierarchical structure composed of functional silos in which only the most senior managers carry profit and loss responsibilities. Those at the lower levels have little visibility of the impact of their contributions and consequently little opportunity to demonstrate their executive potential.

Of the two structural alternatives, the flat structure is the more supportive one in which to implement a talent management strategy.

COMPLEXITY AND CHANGE

BUSINESS AGILITY

The ability to react quickly to changes in market conditions or to exploit emerging opportunities is the hallmark of the agile company.

While strategic decisions to change form and direction will be determined at board level, the changes themselves will need to be implemented within the body of the organization.

One of the desirable qualities for members of the talent pool is the ability to handle change and so the larger the pool the greater the capacity for business agility.

Business change is a four stage process:

1. analysis of the situation

2. determination of the changes required

3. execution of the changes

4. analysis of the impact.

At each stage there will need to be financial calculations about the cost and return. These are non-trivial tasks and require some intellectual capacity to be properly completed.

BUSINESS COMPLEXITY

The need to react to competitive and consumer pressures is a constant corporate challenge. As a result, business processes are becoming increasingly sophisticated often with a high dependence upon complex computerization.

Supply chain management and customer relationship management are two examples of complex computer applications. In the financial services sector, dealing and trading systems are absolutely dependent upon computerization, and the increasing use of e-commerce applications for customer servicing and order fulfilment is having an impact in the retail and distribution sectors.

Complexity, like change, requires a degree of intellectual agility. Significant investments in new computer systems will not deliver the potential benefits unless they are correctly used. In fact, many large investments in this area that are classed as failures can be shown to have only failed because the users did not understand how to use them.

The existence of a pool of intellectually able people who are capable of managing complex processes and introducing sophisticated solutions is a real asset and a further justification for a talent management strategy.

CHANGE CHAMPIONS

Given the need for business agility and the need to handle business complexity on a continuing basis, it seems sensible to recognize that these are inherent aspects of modern corporate life.

One important aspect of change management is that changes have to be developed and implemented while the organization continues to function in its current state.

As a result, some organizations have created separate departments or teams which are charged with securing performance improvements on a continuing basis. These 'change champions' are sourced from within the organization although the team may be supplemented by external specialist consultants.

This is a classic role for members of the talent pool, and periods spent in such teams will be a valuable part of their career development. As members of the team responsible for implementing changes they will also be well positioned to take leading roles in the management of the new processes.

AGILITY AND FLEXIBILITY

SURVIVAL IN A CHANGING WORLD

We saw in the previous section the importance of the need for business agility and the ability to handle business complexity. We also saw the need to have internal resources who could react positively to a changing environment.

The majority of people seek a degree of certainty in their lives. In the workplace they settle into a role and look for ways to accomplish their objectives against a set of performance parameters. When the parameters or processes are changed, life becomes less certain and their competences are tested with a possible consequential loss of confidence.

Change is a necessary part of corporate life and so something must be done to address the human impact.

People will adapt to change more readily providing that the following steps are taken:

- the reason for the change is explained

- training is given in the new processes

- support is provided in the changeover period

- the impact of the change is communicated.

These factors should be included in the terms of reference of the change team or champions because, no matter how beneficial the proposed change will be, it will have little chance of success unless those who are affected by it are able to implement it.

CHANGE – A CHALLENGE OR A PROBLEM

It is important that the corporate culture supports the need for business agility and embraces change as part of corporate life.

The driver for change is the need to find ways to improve performance. Some changes will be quite fundamental and will alter the whole structure of the organization while others will be more in the form of 'fine tuning' to address specific short-term issues. The important consideration is that change is to be expected and seen as a challenge rather than as a problem.

Building an organization which seeks change in order to achieve performance improvement is an executive issue but one which will be based upon the need to employ people who share the same vision and have the ability to embrace new techniques and processes as part of their daily lives.

THE PURSUIT OF PERFORMANCE

At the heart of all change management is the need to improve performance. Change for its own sake has little merit or impact.

Performance improvement will have an eventual impact upon the financial profile of the organization but in many instances the impact may not be a direct one.

In my experience performance improvement is achieved under one of two headings – efficiency and productivity.

- Under efficiency, the challenge is to find or develop processes and practices which will allow people to achieve their objectives more effectively.

- Under productivity, the challenge is to produce the same output through the use of fewer resources. In this case, resources can be finance, people or equipment.

The ability to devise processes and practices that will deliver performance improvement will be a function of the competence of the organization, which will be enhanced by a deliberate policy of recruiting and developing talented resources.

THE RISE OF THE KNOWLEDGE WORKER

BRAINS NOT BRAWN

Modern technology, equipment and industrial plant, not to mention robots, have removed much of the demand for physical strength and manual skills in trade and industry. These resources have largely been replaced by a new workforce called knowledge workers. Even in some of the remaining manual roles there is an element of technical knowledge required in order to operate labour-saving equipment.

Knowledge workers depend upon learned expertise to do their work, and part of the management task is to ensure that the learning process is effective. Those who learn quickest and best will be the superior performers.

One of the key characteristics of a talented individual is a capacity for quick learning and the ability to apply what they have learned in an effective manner. The truly talented are good at being good. They have the capacity to master new knowledge sets and apply them effectively.

The rise of the knowledge worker is an important dimension of modern business. The old practices of learning a trade and using it for life are now in the past.

MAINTAINING KNOWLEDGE LEVELS

If knowledge is the key characteristic of the knowledge worker, then there is a requirement to keep it relevant and current. Technology now plays an important part in most business processes not least demonstrated by the ubiquitous computer and other electronic gadgetry.

Technology and its application do not stand still and so there is a demand for continuous updating of technical skills in order to fully exploit the available potential.

A 'learning' company is one which recognizes their dependence upon the competence levels of the knowledge workers and takes appropriate steps to ensure that appropriate training programmes are in place.

Those in the talent pool will require particular attention because, by virtue of their membership of that group, they have the capacity to quickly absorb new ideas and so will become the champions for new processes.

MANAGING KNOWLEDGE WORKERS

One of the problems with developing knowledge levels in knowledge workers is determining what levels of knowledge they should have.

For any specific role or function there will be a body of knowledge that is required in order to perform the role effectively. This body of knowledge may then be divided into a number of competencies in each of which the individual is required to have knowledge and ability.

In Chapter 4 we explore the application of knowledge assessment in more detail, but the essential elements are:

- define the body of knowledge that is required

- assess the levels that exist

- identify where the knowledge gaps lie

- deliver training and education to fill the gaps.

The overall objective is to ensure that human resources have sufficient levels of knowledge to be able to adequately perform their roles.

TALENTED KNOWLEDGE WORKERS

Members of the talent pool are also knowledge workers and so are subject to the same assessment procedures as other members of staff. They may have a capacity for quicker learning and may be more effective in applying their knowledge. If so, they can play a further role in terms of sharing some of the training load.

We have found that one of the true tests of knowledge about a subject is the ability to transfer that knowledge to others in a structured and coherent form. We would certainly encourage the concept that members of the talent pool should be required to spend some time in training roles and receive some training in how to conduct knowledge transfer assignments.

BUILDING THE CORPORATE BRAND

BUILDING BRAND SOUL

Brand soul is a marketing term used to describe the inherent qualities and characteristics of an organization. It is not an artificial construct added as a layer to the image presentation of the organization. It reflects the real essence of it.

It comprises three elements:

1. vision – what the company wants to achieve and how it wants to be perceived

2. passion – what it is good at and how excellence is manifested

3. culture – its core values and the way in which it operates.

Those organizations that have a strong brand soul are those where these elements are clearly articulated and, more importantly, they are understood by and shared by everyone in the organization.

Brand soul is at the heart of building a strong corporate brand. If the people are the company then the people must subscribe to the elements which constitute its soul.

A COMPANY TO WORK FOR

Good people want to work for good companies and so building a brand image that attracts both customers and employees is a wise investment.

Prospective employees, if they have any ability, will want to know about opportunities for personal and career development and how these opportunities are structured and supported. The existence of a formal talent management strategy will do much to attract the interest of able people.

While the compensation plan and benefits package play an important element in attracting potential employees of the right calibre, it will not be the exclusive driver. The existence of a clearly articulated brand soul not only helps in attracting good candidates; it also helps in selecting those who will fit into the culture and make an impact.

Any talent management strategy depends for its success on recruiting and retaining high performers. This needs to start at the beginning with the recruitment and selection process; in this way, every opportunity of making the organization one which people want to work for should be exploited to the full.

A COMPANY TO STAY WITH

After recruitment, retention is the second biggest issue for the talent management strategy.

Individuals who join an organization on the basis that it will provide an opportunity for personal and career development, together with accelerated promotion prospects for high fliers will quickly become disillusioned if there are no demonstrations of the delivery of these promises.

The tone needs to be set in the induction process in which there is an opportunity to reinforce the propositions made at the selection stage and to demonstrate in what ways the promises will be delivered against.

For those recruits who are identified as potential members of the talent pool, the identification of coaches and possibly mentors will further support the recruitment propositions.

In interviews with senior executives about their early careers, one of the points we discussed was the way that they were introduced into their organizations.

Some characterized their induction process as being tantamount to being thrown into the deep end to see if they could swim. Others described their induction process as being a formative experience which really built a bond with their employer.

Of the two alternatives it was obvious which one they had gained most value from.

BUILDING FOR THE FUTURE

The talent pool is designed to be the source of future senior executives. Developing a cohort of rounded and competent managers who can take on senior responsibilities takes time and may not produce the required skills sets at the right time.

Where specific skills are required which cannot be satisfied from internal resources, there will be the need to resort to external recruitment to fill the gap. This action can be seen as either a threat or criticism to internal resources and must be handled with some care.

Senior appointments from external resources bring a number of advantages, not least being the injection of new blood and a fresh approach, but they can be seen as a negative comment from the perspective of internal resources. It is important to show that such actions are not an obstruction of internal resources or a comment on their capabilities but rather a tactical action designed to solve a specific problem.

TALENT MANAGEMENT IN A DYNAMIC ENVIRONMENT

INTRODUCTION

Organizations operate in a dynamic environment. As we have seen, a capacity to live with change is one of the desirable characteristics of members of the talent pool.

Many requirements for organizational and operational change are imposed by external factors such as competition, legislation or technology. These are reactive changes over which the organization may have little control.

On the other hand, there are proactive changes, those which are generated by actions or decisions made by choice of the organization itself. In this section we want to look at how the availability of a talent pool can assist in the execution of changes in this category.

ACCELERATED GROWTH

There will be periods in the development of an organization where market conditions are such that they will support a strategy of accelerated growth. Rapid expansion puts stress on the corporate infrastructure, not least upon the capabilities and competencies of human capital.

Where such a strategy is adopted we believe it is important to identify individuals who have the capability to handle the increased pressures and who can take key roles in the expansion programme.

Accelerated revenue growth, accompanied by resource growth, will increase the critical mass of the organization but do little to increase the operating margin. In my experience the pursuit of accelerated growth should also be accompanied by a drive for productivity improvement so that both revenues and profiles are improved.

To achieve these twin objectives it is necessary to undertake some preliminary planning which investigates not only what can be achieved but how it can be achieved with improved efficiency. These should be the terms of reference of the expansion planning team, the composition of which requires the injection of talented resources.

MERGERS AND ACQUISITIONS

While organic growth is the normal route for organization expansion, accelerated growth can be obtained through selected mergers and acquisitions.

Financial due diligence will be a necessary part of the acquisition process, but we think it is also important to conduct a parallel assessment of the human capital in the target organization. In our experience this consideration is rarely given the attention it deserves.

Anecdotal evidence suggests that few acquisitions deliver the expected range of benefits. In my experience, while considerable energy and expertise are devoted to the acquisition process, relatively little is devoted to acquisition integration and the actions that are needed in order to secure the target benefits.

At the core of this challenge is the need to integrate possibly different cultures, processes and practices but, more importantly, there is the need to recognize the impact of an acquisition upon the human resources in the acquired company.

One approach that we have found to be particularly successful is to create an integration team made up of selected members from both organizations. This team will have a specific set of objectives and a fixed life span. If, during the acquisition process, there has been an assessment of the human capital capabilities of the target company, it will be possible to identify candidates for the integration team. The assessment should also have the objective of identifying potential members of the combined talent pool.

DOWNSIZING AND RETRENCHMENT

Economic and trade cycles will occasionally require that organizations reduce in size in order to keep the cost base in line with the revenue stream.

When such actions become necessary, the question arises about how to conduct the retrenchment without doing serious damage to the organization, often described as 'cutting out the fat without removing the muscle'.

Downsizing is an unpleasant business but, when it is necessary for survival, it has to be done. Not surprisingly it has a negative effect upon morale in the organization as people become aware that their jobs may be vulnerable. Where headcount has to be reduced we have found it useful to adopt an 'averaging up' approach which is designed to ensure that we retain the high achievers at the expense of low or average performers.

Those in the talent pool need special attention as they may see the retrenchment as a curtailment of their career potential. They are also the people who will find it easier to find jobs in other organizations. When times are difficult it is important to keep the high achievers in the organization because they are the people who will be most needed in implementing the survival and recovering programmes.

SUMMARY

In this Chapter we have looked at a range of situations in which a talent management strategy will provide the resources needed to address a number of operational challenges and opportunities.

There is no doubt that the ability to draw upon a pool of high achievers is a significant organizational advantage and we hope that the previous sections have demonstrated that point.

A deliberate and strategic objective of recruiting, developing and retaining a pool of really talented individuals is an investment that will pay handsome dividends.

CASE STUDIES

CASE STUDY 1: BUILDING A WORLD-CLASS SALES FORCE

The situation

An international computer services company had analysed market trends and was predicting a period of sustained and rapid growth in its target markets. It believed that delivery capacity could be expanded significantly through selective acquisitions but recognized that serious investments would be needed to create a sales force capable of delivering the growth plans.

Key issues

The current sales force had developed through a process of recruitment and internal sourcing. The competency spread ranged from outstanding to barely acceptable. Overall performance was patchy and did not provide a platform in which the Directors had confidence.

One of the problems lay in the diverse nature of the sales force: those who had been recruited from outside had brought their own practices and processes and had been allowed to continue to use them provided that they achieved their sales targets. Internal recruits to the sales force had attended a proprietary sales training programme and had then been allocated their territories.

Problems to overcome

An analysis of the situation identified the following problem areas:

- wide range in individual sales performance

- performance appraisal was driven by sales target achievement only

- no consistency in sales process or practice

- wide variations in sales forecasting accuracy

- no coherent way of identifying potential sales managers

- no training programme for sales managers

- no defined process for the interview process for new sales recruits.

All of these factors contributed towards an executive impression that the overall sales function was out of control and that serious actions needed to be taken to remedy the situation.

The solution

It was decided to employ a specialist sales performance consultant who would conduct a detailed analysis of the current situation and make specific recommendations. The report was comprehensive and direct. The executive board decided to implement the majority of the recommendations but added a new twist – they decided that they wanted to develop a world-class sales force and were prepared to devote time and money towards the achievement of this objective.

The sales performance consultant was retained as an adviser for the duration of the project.

The initial project planning involved the definition of the project objectives; they included the following:

- All members of the sales force will have proven aptitude for their role.

- All members of the sales force will have adequate professional knowledge to perform their role.

- Annual assessments will take into account aptitude and knowledge as well as performance measures.

- Deficiencies in measured knowledge levels will be remedied by focused training and measurement of the training impact.

- A standard sales process will be selected, adopted and implemented.

- Sales forecasting accuracy will be improved and individual performance will be assessed at the annual performance review.

- All sales people will receive education and training in the features and benefits propositions of the relevant elements of the service offer portfolio.

- All sales people will receive training in the commercial elements of bid management, the pricing strategy and the legal requirements of proposals and contracts.

What the executive directors wanted to build was a sales force that was fully trained and which performed in a predictable and consistent manner.

One of the first activities was a pruning and tuning programme. In this, each current member of the sales force undertook a knowledge assessment to measure their knowledge of sales processes and techniques. Those who scored badly and had a poor performance record left the company. Those who had a medium combination of knowledge and ability were earmarked for specific training courses and put on notice that their performance required improvement. The top performers carried on without short-term corrective programmes.

A separate programme was developed to recruit additions to the sales force. Three streams were developed:

1. The recruitment of external candidates who could pass the new selection process for experienced sales people.

2. The identification of internal candidates who could pass the aptitude tests and who showed sales potential.

3. The recruitment of external candidates with no sales experience but who could pass the aptitude tests and recruitment procedures.

One key element of the programme was the use of psychometric tests to assess sales aptitude and knowledge assessments to measure knowledge levels in the required sales competency areas.

These tests and assessments were included in the new interview and selection procedures as well as for the pruning and tuning exercise applied to existing members of the sales force.

A further development was the introduction of a grading structure of the sales force. Three grades were introduced with specific definitions of the capabilities required to be allocated to a particular grade. The sales grades were:

- sales executives – for high achievers with a proven track record and who had achieved high scores in the assessment process

- sales professionals – competent performers who showed potential to become sales executives but who had not yet demonstrated consistent performance

- sales trainees – aspirant sales people who showed aptitude and who would be subject to intensive training and mentoring for their first 12 months.

A sales training programme was developed and introduced; some of the training was supplied by external training companies.

The training programme focused on three key areas:

- The use of a structured sales process and training in selling techniques;

- Specific focus on opportunity qualification and sales forecasting;

- Product and service training together with the development of commercial awareness.

Outcome and benefits achieved

Over the first 12 months of the programme there was a certain amount of internal upheaval. About 20 per cent of the original sales force left the company as a result of the pruning programme. New recruits who had passed the new selection procedures, and were supplemented by staff from acquired companies who could meet the new standards, filled these gaps.

A group of sales trainees was recruited – mainly university graduates and ex-military officers. They spent their first three months at sales school and were then assigned to sales executives who became their mentors and coaches. After six months their performance was assessed and some fell by the wayside. At the end of the 12-month training programme the majority were appointed as sales professionals.

Performance metrics had been set at the outset and were measured carefully in the 12-month period. The performance metrics included:

- length of the sales cycle

- accuracy of sales forecasting

- conversion rates at selected points in the sales process

- average order size

- achievement of sales targets.

Every member of the sales force was assessed on these measures every month. The objective was to emphasize the need to deliver improved performance and that these metrics were important.

It took some time for the programme to settle in but, after three months, there began to be a steady improvement in most areas and, by the end of the year, the sponsoring executive was able to demonstrate that the investment was producing the desired results.

Re-enforcement programme

The selection and interview process, which combined aptitude and knowledge assessments, was reviewed with the objective of identifying other techniques that could help to pinpoint candidates who would deliver superior results. Additions included ways of identifying desirable soft skills, leadership potential and stress management capabilities.

The training programme was expanded to include training in various soft skills and time management.

Promotion from sales professional to sales executive was formalized with the introduction of a promotion panel and a more precise set of promotion criteria. The objective was to build a sales force in which 60 per cent were at the sales executive level.

Sales managers were appointed from the sales executive pool and were given advanced training before taking up their new roles.

CASE STUDY 2: SUCCESSION PLANNING

The situation

The newly appointed CEO of a large manufacturing company adopted the standard 'first 100 days' strategy for reviewing the situation and setting his goals and objectives.

He divided his action planning into three time bands – short-, medium- and long-term issues. Within the short-term plan he commissioned a study of the capabilities of the middle and senior management grades; his primary objective was to find out what management material he had to work with.

Key issues

The resulting report, prepared by an external firm of HR consultants, painted a rather depressing picture. Among the findings was a profile of the length of service of the senior management team. On average they had worked for the company for less than five years and over 30 per cent had less than three years' experience with the company.

This demonstrated an alarmingly high rate of senior management turnover and raised the natural question as to the cause of this situation. This was compounded by the fact, already known by the CEO, that each of his three predecessors had had tenure in office of less than three years and all had been external appointments.

The consultancy report also identified that one of the largest budget items for the HR department was fees paid to search firms for replacing departed executives. The CEO decided to make succession planning a strategic issue and one of the planks on which he would make a personal impact upon company performance.

Problems to overcome

The key problem was that managers in the middle ranks had not been seen to be potential candidates for promotion to the senior grades. As a result the majority of senior executive jobs were filled by external appointees. This practice did not go unnoticed by those in the middle ranks who consequently decided to advance their careers by leaving and joining other companies. Only those of above-average ability were able to take this action, with a consequent drain on internal competence potential.

The practice of filling senior roles through external appointments introduced a number of other problems. The new recruits took time to adapt to their new roles; they introduced new practices (some of which created internal turmoil); they built teams mainly comprising people from their previous jobs (which further antagonized current employees); and many failed to produce the expected performance improvements and subsequently departed only to result in a repeat of the cycle.

Clearly this was an unsustainable situation and had to be given serious attention. Equally clearly the problem could not be solved overnight; it would take time to remedy the situation and the CEO knew that time was not on his side.

The solution

The CEO decided to make this a board issue; he recognized that he would have to build a business case which would support an investment programme and a fundamental change in approach to human capital. He recognized that the business case would need to be evidence based and so he created a small project team which had the following terms of reference:

- to identify the direct and indirect historical costs of filling senior posts through external recruiting;

- to identify the impact of high rates of turnover in the middle management ranks;

- to identify what actions would be required in order to develop middle management capabilities to a point where candidates could be identified for promotion to senior grades;

- to develop an outline programme which would address these issues and identify the cost implications.

The resultant report included a strong recommendation to adopt a talent management strategy which had the primary objective of developing a pool of able candidates for promotion to senior roles – the emphasis was very strongly on succession planning.

However, the report went further and approached the problem from first principles and looked at how the calibre of staff joining the company at the entry level could be improved, the objective being to attract graduate entrants with high potential who would form the basis of the future management pool.

Outcome and benefits achieved

The report was accepted by the board and an expanded project team, led by the HR Director, was established to implement the recommendations. The programme was given extensive internal publicity with direct support from the CEO. A staff attitude study showed that the programme was greeted with cautious enthusiasm – the main concern being 'let's see if it works in reality'. To counter this scepticism each part of the programme was introduced by the CEO as a demonstration that the strategy was being implemented as planned.

In order to give real impetus to the programme, particular attention was paid to the middle management grades with the objective of identifying those with the potential to move to greater responsibilities. The members of this group were identified and each allocated a mentor who became responsible for managing their career development.

A further development was to ask each senior executive to identify a potential successor from within the company and decide what training, experience and capabilities would be needed to equip that individual to take on that role.

As anticipated by the CEO, the programme took some time to begin to deliver quantifiable results; he also had many other problems to contend with. However, the introduction of the programme had a measurable effect upon staff morale which certainly helped with the execution of the other changes he wanted to make.

The first 100 days is a testing period for any incoming CEO, but attention to human capital issues seems to be high on the list of necessary actions. In this case it proved to be so, and provided a platform from which to make a valuable contribution as well as making a very visible impact.

CHAPTER 3

Elements of Psychometric Testing

INTRODUCTION

In this Chapter we will look at psychometric testing. It is a term that covers a variety of assessment techniques. The British Psychological Society uses the following definition:

> A psychological test is any procedure on the basis of which inferences are made concerning a person's capacity, propensity or liability to act, react, experience, or to structure or order thought or behaviour in particular ways.

Psychological tests cover three distinct aspects of people's future behaviour:

- aptitude – the differences in their ability to perform or carry out different tasks;

- personality – the differences in their style or manner of doing things, and in the way they interact with their environment and other people;

- attitude – the differences in their motivation, in the direction and strength of their interests, and in their values and opinions.

As such, psychometric tests are therefore used in a predictive way and give an insight into future activity. There is another category of assessments that measure knowledge already attained. At their simplest they could be a series of questions designed to find out a basic knowledge of, say, arithmetic, or grammar. At their most sophisticated they are known as knowledge assessments; these make an assessment against a recognized 'body of knowledge' pertaining to a particular job function. We will examine these in detail in Chapter 4.

HOW DID THE NEED ARISE?

The first psychometric instruments were basically aptitude tests designed to measure the concept of intelligence. A high intelligence was considered to be a predictive indicator of the ability to deliver superior results in the work environment. The best known historical approach involves the Stanford-Binet

IQ test, developed originally by the French psychologist Alfred Binet and amended by Robert Yerkes of Stanford University. This was used by Yerkes as the basis of Army selection in World War I when over 1 million US servicemen took the Army Alpha or Army Beta tests. The scores dictated whether one would be an officer, a serviceman or rejected altogether. This was an early attempt at talent management.

Another major focus in psychometrics has been on personality testing.

There have been a range of theoretical approaches to conceptualizing and measuring personality. Some of the better known instruments include the Minnesota Multiphasic Personality Inventory (MMPI) and the Myers-Briggs Type Indicator (MBTI).

MMPI is the most frequently used personality test in the mental health field. This assessment or test was designed to help identify personal, social and behavioural problems in psychiatric patients. This test helps provide relevant information to aid in problem identification, diagnosis and treatment planning for the patient.

In the non-medical field one of the early assessments was the Myers-Briggs Type Indicator which is a personality test designed to assist a person in identifying their personality preferences. Developed by Katharine Cook Briggs and her daughter Isabel Briggs Myers during World War II, it follows on from the theories of Carl Jung as laid out in his work *Psychological Types*. The personality types identified by the MBTI, known as dichotomies, are extroversion/introversion, sensing/intuition, thinking/feeling and judging/perceiving. Participants are given one of 16 four-letter acronyms, such as ESTJ or INFP, where each letter indicates their preferred style of operating in that particular dichotomy.

Initially Myers asserted that because each type has unique strengths, no type is superior to another.[1] However, after further reflection it is clear that she recognized that the unique attributes of each type enable them to excel in certain situations. Consequently there has been much derivative research based on MBTI that maintains that certain profiles are more suited to particular types of employment roles than others.

Attitudes have also been studied extensively in psychometrics. A common approach to the measurement of attitudes is the use of the Likert Scale. It

1   Isabel Briggs-Myers (with Peter Myers), *Gifts Differing*, Consulting Psychologists Press, 1980.

was named after Rensis Likert, the American educator and organizational psychologist, who invented the scale in 1932. A typical test item in a Likert scale is a statement that the respondent is asked to indicate their degree of agreement with. Traditionally a five-point scale is used; however, many psychometricians advocate using a seven- or nine-point scale. Here is an example where the respondents are asked to circle where on the scale they judge themselves to be in relation to the statement:

I prefer to work alone

1. Strongly disagree

2. Disagree

3. Neither agree nor disagree

4. Agree

5. Strongly agree.

Thus, Likert scaling is a method that measures either positive or negative response to a statement. Sometimes Likert scales are used in a forced-choice mode where the middle option of 'Neither agree nor disagree' is not available.

Once the questionnaire is completed the scores on each item are summed together, to create a test score for person. Therefore Likert scales are often also known as summative scales.

WHAT ARE PSYCHOMETRIC TESTS?

ATTITUDE/ABILITY TESTS

The aptitudes most commonly tested are different aspects of critical reasoning. The fields most commonly tested are verbal and numerical abilities, since they are core elements of most graduate jobs. Other categories include diagrammatic, which involves logical reasoning based on abstract symbols; spatial, which requires the visualization of two- and three-dimensional shapes in space; and mechanical, where relevant problems are shown in pictorial form.

An aptitude test has a formal, structured procedure. It is given under examination conditions and is strictly timed. Most tests use the multi-choice answer technique, where you shade in, cross or tick the box against the correct answer (there is only ever one correct answer).

The test will be standardized in terms of the way it is administered and in the way it is scored. This allows your result to be compared to others.

PERSONALITY ASSESSMENTS

This second type is, strictly speaking, not really a test, as there are no right or wrong answers. There are a wide variety of 'personality' assessments available. However, as the approach to personality differs widely (see below) great care must be taken when choosing which personality assessments to use in a talent management programme.

A DEFINITION OF PERSONALITY

Goodstein and Lanyon's (1975) definition of personality is:

> *the enduring characteristics of the person that are significant for interpersonal behaviour*[2]

Within this general definition a number of different theoretical approaches exist:

- the psychometric approach (Eysenck and Cattell)
- the psychodynamic approach (Freud, Jung, Adler)
- the social learning approach (Mischel, Bandura)
- the humanistic approach (Maslow, Rogers).

These approaches to personality are theoretically very different and such a diversity of theories exist because personality is a hypothetical construct which can never be directly observed but only inferred from behaviour.

ATTITUDE ASSESSMENTS

This third type is also not a test because there are no right or wrong answers. When employers assess an individual's preferences for different types of work activity, their opinions and attitudes, or how they tend to react and behave towards others, their interest lies in the candidate's usual way of approaching situations or people. Interests and values are usually assessed by means of questionnaires without time limits. The patterns that emerge are interpreted by the assessor, who will normally have had to undertake training to ensure that the interpretation and subsequent feedback is accurate.

---

2   Leonard D. Goldstein and Richard I. Lanyon, *Adjustment, Behaviour, and Personality*, Addison-Wesley, 1975.

AUDIENCE

According to a UK online recruitment consultancy, a recent study said that 87 per cent of employers now use psychometric tests when recruiting. However, not all of these companies will be considered exemplars when it comes to talent management. So even to keep up with best practice in some mediocre companies, psychometric tests will need to be used when recruiting, from the school leaver entering into business for the first time right up to the most senior managers.

There are a number of ways to reach the best practice level for talent management using psychometric tests.

Firstly, pick the most appropriate psychometric tests for the job in hand. Some aptitude tests are designed specifically for the school leaver. The Basic Skills Agency – Initial Assessment of Literacy and Numeracy is an example. This is described in more detail later in this Chapter.

However, when hiring an executive level manager many of the top organizations will use industrial psychologists to assist with the recruitment. These psychologists will often subject the executive to a series of aptitude, personality and attitude assessments, together with an extensive interview. The subsequent reports will measure, amongst other things:

- intellectual capacity (IQ)
- emotional maturity (EQ)
- communication ability
- self-awareness
- determination and energy.

Secondly, compare the results of each type of assessment against the profile of existing employees who are considered to be exemplars for the role being recruited. This will be done in addition to the knowledge assessment and the interview to ascertain the degree of organizational fit the applicant has. Microsoft, one of the world's best performing companies, insists that not recruiting is more preferable than recruiting a 'near fit' against its various requirements measurement. Psychometric tests can therefore play a powerful role in answering the question 'how well does the applicant match the culture and values of our organization?'

Thirdly, in order to bring psychometric tests to the fore in a talent management setting it is not good enough to use them only when recruiting but also throughout the life of the individual's employment with you.

There are many areas where psychometric tests will help with the development of talent over the course of a number of years. The objective of this is twofold: to increase the employee's contribution to the company and equally as important to keep the employee motivated by the fact that they are developing themselves, and therefore their CVs. Although this latter point may seem contradictory, top organizations recognize that if they do not help their talent to improve their employability to other organizations they will lose them to employers who do.

POPULAR PSYCHOMETRIC TESTS

The following is a sample of some of the more popular of the thousands of psychometric tests that are now available.

MYERS-BRIGGS TYPE INDICATOR

The Myers-Briggs Type Indicator has already been referred to above, and demonstrates personal response style. It shows the individual's preferences on four scales, where each scale represents two opposing preferences. To understand the concept of preferences it is useful to use the analogy of right- and left-handedness. Here is an opportunity for a practical session. Write your name with each hand. You will notice that with your preferred hand it was an easy task and one that did not require much effort or concentration. With the non-preferred hand, however, it required more effort, more concentration and took longer and probably produced a less readable result! It should not be forgotten, though, that most people *can* write with both hands, so the same is true with the MBTI preferences: what the profile predicts is your preferred way of thinking and acting; it does not say that you can never operate in the non-preferred mode.

The four scales are:

1. Where you focus your attention – the extroversion/introversion scale.

2. How you acquire information – the sensing/intuition scale.

3. How you make decisions and form opinions – the thinking/feeling scale.

4. How you interact with the outside world – the judging/perceiving scale.

There are detailed analyses of the 16 types that this technique produces, but for our purposes here it is enough to say that there are four broad categories, being: sensors, intuitors, thinkers and feelers.

How can this help the individual and the organization? Well, firstly an organization will need a combination of all of these people; intuitors provide a clear sense of direction, sensors bring realism and practicality, thinkers provide analysis and consequences, and feelers will be able to forecast how people will respond to events and initiatives. Secondly, for an individual, it is helpful to understand that one's preferences indicate what areas of the job and management come more easily than others. Also, it will help with the insight that extra effort will be needed when working in a non-preferred role.

It is also helpful for an individual to recognize that not everybody thinks in the same way. This has an impact on one-to-one communication. If there are certain people who find it difficult to communicate with each other it is likely that their MBTI profiles do not match. It also has importance for team working. While each effective team will need some elements of sensing, intuiting, feeling and thinking, by their very nature the individuals with these traits will not be thinking on the same wavelength.

HONEY AND MUMFORD LEARNING STYLES

Honey and Mumford, two British psychologists, in 1992 developed a very popular learning styles questionnaire, which categorized people by their preferred learning styles:

- *Activists*: are people who involve themselves in new learning experiences. They are open-minded rather than sceptical and will 'try anything once'. They love fire fighting and crisis management but get bored by repetition.

- *Reflectors*: like to stand back to ponder experiences and consider them from many different perspectives. They collect data both first and second hand and prefer to think about it thoroughly before coming to any conclusions. In meetings they will tend to listen rather than speak, as they take a long time to make up their minds.

- *Theorists*: are people who adapt and integrate their observations into complex but logically sound theories. They think problems through in a vertical, step-by-step, logical way. They also tend to be perfectionists who will not rest until they have suitable rational explanations for things that they are working on.

- *Pragmatists*: are keen on anything that works in practice. They positively search out new ideas and take the first opportunity to experiment with applications. They tend to be impatient with ruminating and open-ended discussions.

Understanding how an individual learns is key to identifying how best to educate them in their employment, be it product and service knowledge, compliance issues or new managerial approaches. Clearly this has cost and time implications for the company.

Much effort is made by organizations to deliver education and training via internal workshops and training courses. Below are listed how each of the four types would prefer the courses to be run:

Activist:

- I want to learn new things
- There must be lots of different activities
- I don't want to be just sitting and listening for hours
- It should be lots of fun
- I hope there are other like-minded people there
- There must be problems to solve.

Reflectors:

- I want to know what I need to prepare for the course
- There must be lots of time to consider and assimilate during the course
- Everybody should be given a chance to offer their opinions and ideas
- There must be plenty of time to gain relevant information.

Theorists:

- I want to be able to ask lots of questions
- There needs to be clear objectives and structure to the course
- Complex and stretching ideas should be generated
- All ideas put forward need to be proven and respectable
- I hope there are other high-calibre people there.

Pragmatists:

- I need to be able to practise and experiment with the ideas mooted

- The course should address the real needs of the organization

- I want plenty of practical tips and techniques

- I need to be taught by experts who can do it themselves.

Of course the question is whether one course can ever fulfil all of the above requirements. Honey and Mumford argue that there is also an onus on the individual to improve their non-preferred styles of learning as well so that they do benefit from as many learning opportunities as possible.

BELBIN'S TEAM ROLES

Dr R. Meredith Belbin studied teams at the Henley Management College. He defines a team role as 'our tendency to behave, contribute and interrelate with others in a particular way'.

He identified nine different sorts of roles, listed below.

- *Plant*: advances new ideas and strategies with special attention to the major issues facing the team. They look for possible changes in approach to the problem that the group is confronting. A plant encourages the team to think laterally.

- *Resource Investigator*: explores and reports on ideas, developments and resources outside the group that may help the team, and also takes the team's work to the outside world. This means creating external contacts that will be useful to the team.

- *Co-ordinator*: controls the way in which the team moves forward towards the group objectives by making the best use of team resources. This person recognizes where the team's strengths and weaknesses lie and ensures that best use is made of each member's potential.

- *Shaper*: shapes the way the team effort is applied by directing attention generally to the setting of objectives and priorities. He or she will also impose some shape or pattern on group discussions and on the outcomes of group activities.

- *Monitor/Evaluator:* analyses problems, evaluates ideas and suggestions so that the team is better placed to take balanced decisions.

- *Team Worker:* supports other members of the teams and builds on their contributions. They improve communication and build team spirit.

- *Company Worker (also known as Implementer):* turns concepts and plans into practical working procedures.

- *Completer/Finisher*: ensures the team is protected as far as possible from mistakes of both commission and omission. He or she searches for aspects of work that need a more than usual degree of attention; and maintains a sense of urgency within the team.

- *Specialist*: brings technical information into the group but does not contribute to the team dynamic.

As with the MBTI profile above, the importance of understanding an employee's preferred team role is twofold.

Firstly, to create highly effective teams you need a balance of preferred roles, and secondly, the individual will benefit from realizing that the other team members have different strengths, and weaknesses, to their own.

A balanced team could look like:

- the leader being a Co-ordinator or Shaper

- a Plant for new ideas (more than one may create too many new ideas)

- a Monitor/Evaluator to maintain clarity and direction

- one or more Company Worker, Resource Investigator, Team Worker or Completer/Finisher to ensure that the work gets done.

So once again, at recruitment time and when forming new teams from existing employees, knowledge of their MBTI and Belbin profiles will be of great assistance.

SAVILLE AND HOLDSWORTH OCCUPATIONAL PERSONALITY QUESTIONNAIRE®

Saville and Holdsworth (SHL) was originally a British company of psychologists that now operates on a worldwide basis. It launched its flagship product, the Occupational Personality Questionnaire® (OPQ), in 1984. It has since become one of the world's best known personality questionnaires.

The latest version, OPQ32, has many business applications and in addition to being used in the recruitment process SHL also say that it can assist in the following areas:

- identify future leaders

- re-deploy talent across the business

- recommend senior managers for cross-border engagements

- evaluate the talent pool following a merger/acquisition/restructure

- create a project team

- manage the transformation of a technical specialist to an effective people manager.

The latest version, OPQ32, assesses job competencies based on 32 specific personality characteristics. These characteristics fall within the three categories of: Relationship with People, Thinking Style, and Feelings and Emotions.

For example, the Feelings and Emotions category is further broken down into Emotions and Dynamism, and within Dynamism the characteristics measured are: Vigorous, Competitive, Achieving and Decisive.

It is the combination of these 32 dimensions which influence performance against the key job competencies. The OPQ32 provides detailed competency reporting against the 20 key competencies from the Universal Competency Framework™ that SHL developed, which was launched in 2003.

SIXTEEN PERSONALITY FACTOR QUESTIONNAIRE (16PF5)

The 16PF5 questionnaire is the fifth version of the 16PF, originally devised in 1949 by Dr Raymond Cattell as part of his work to identify the primary components of personality.

The 16PF is designed to give a broad measure of personality that is useful to practitioners in a wide range of settings: from selection, to counselling, to clinical decision-making.

The 16PF5 was constructed by the Institute for Personality and Ability Testing (IPAT) in the USA, who also collected US normative data on a sample of 2500 persons. (IPAT is now owned by the English company OPP.) The American 16PF5 was Anglicised by ASE who changed 36 items. UK normative data have been collected by ASE on a sample of 1322 persons. The 16PF5 is designed for use with adults, defined as those of 16 years and above. Unlike previous versions there is now only one form of the questionnaire. The 16PF5 has 185 items, and measures 16 personality factors known as the primary factors. These are:

A – Warmth	H – Social boldness	Q1 – Openness to change
B – Reasoning	I – Sensitivity	Q2 – Self-reliance
C – Emotional stability	L – Vigilance	Q3 – Perfectionism
E – Dominance	M – Abstractedness	Q4 – Tension
F – Liveliness	N – Privateness	
G – Rule-consciousness	O – Apprehension	

These traits can also be grouped into the following Big 5 Global Factors:

Big 5 Global Factors:
Extroversion
Stability (Anxiety)
Receptivity (Tough-mindedness)
Accommodating (Independence)
Self-control

The participant feedback includes an assessment of personal strengths, including problem-solving resources, patterns of coping with stressful conditions and interpersonal interaction style. It also offers insight into leadership style and aspects of work of interest to the participant, such as influencing, organizing, helping and analysing.

WILL SCHUTZ – THE FIRO-B® QUESTIONNAIRE

The *FIRO-B®* questionnaire, which has been in use since the 1950s, gives valuable insights into the needs individuals bring to their relationships with other people, analysing three key factors – Inclusion, Control and Affection. The instrument is used for both team leadership and individual development, by helping people become more aware of how they relate to others. The aim is then to encourage them to be more flexible in their approach. The results show that it engenders more positive and productive working relationships. The instrument measures how a person typically behaves towards others and how they would like others to behave towards them. It assesses interpersonal style, and its appropriateness in relationships, on three levels: Inclusion, Control and Affection, as shown below:

Inclusion	Control	Affection
Expressed	Expressed	Expressed
I make an effort to include others in my activities. I try to belong, to join social groups – to be with people as much as possible.	I try to exert control and influence over things. I enjoy organizing things and directing others.	I make an effort to get close to people. I am comfortable expressing personal feelings and I try to be supportive of others.
Wanted	Wanted	Wanted
I want other people to invite me to belong. I enjoy it when others notice me.	I feel most comfortable working in well-defined situations. I try to get clear expectations and instructions.	I want others to act warmly towards me. I enjoy it when people share their feelings with me and when they encourage my efforts.

It can be used for the following applications:

- Team building and development:

  – indicating likely sources of compatibility or tension between team members

  – identifying leadership style.

- Aiding effective decision-making:

  – improving communication, openness and trust between colleagues

  – improving conflict resolution.

- Individual development:

  – increasing self-awareness

  – increasing interpersonal effectiveness

  – career development

  – personal growth.

- Relationship counselling:

  – identifying and resolving possible sources of incompatibility and dissatisfaction.

- Selection and placement:

  – helping to structure interviews

  – helping to assess likely team roles or interpersonal behaviour.

SAVILLE AND HOLDSWORTH – ABILITY SCREENING ONLINE (ASO)

This uses Internet technology to present an ability test that has been developed with the rigour that Saville and Holdsworth (SHL) always applies to its psychometric tools. ASO measures the candidates' verbal and numerical reasoning abilities. Clearly it will be used with a variety of other tools (see below); however, it can provide organizations with a fast and efficient method of screening applicants at the earliest stage of the recruitment process, without them ever even attending an interview. This will save time for both the candidate and the organization, and in the organization's case should also save money. By 2006 over 500,000 ASOs from SHL had been sold.

DR STEVE BLINKHORN AND PRD LTD – MODERN OCCUPATIONAL SKILLS TESTS (MOST)

Talent management is about getting and retaining the best people most suited to their jobs. It should therefore apply to all levels in an organization. To assist with this, MOST is a widely used test at the recruitment stage for clerical and junior management positions.

It is a series of nine tests that are divided into three levels of difficulty.

The first level deals with basic office skills covering verbal checking, which measures the ability to detect errors in text; numerical checking, which measures the ability to detect errors in numerical data; and finally, filing, which measures the ability to insert records into the right place.

The second level moves up to an intermediate range of tasks, comprising numerical awareness, which measures arithmetic skills, including the detection and then correction of errors; spelling and grammar, which measures the ability to detect spelling and grammatical errors; and finally, word meanings, which measures sentence comprehension and word choice.

Again moving up, level three checks the specific skills necessary for higher clerical and junior management positions. This comprises: numerical estimation, which measures the ability to make quick and rough approximations to confirm calculations; technical checking, which measures the ability to detect errors when information changes format; and decision-making, which measures the ability to understand and apply rules, regulations and criteria for making choices.

There is a checklist of job tasks, for example, 'sorting correspondence', 'calculating costs and prices', which can be used by the assessor to select which of the nine tests are relevant. Usually a maximum of four tests will be necessary for any one occupation.

As an example of verbal checking, the candidate might be shown some handwritten text and then the same information in a typed format. The candidate has to assess how many errors are in the typed version.

An example of a numerical reasoning question might be a restaurant bill with the items ordered and their prices, where the candidate has to correct the calculations already made and then add in extra calculations to come to the correct bill total.

THE BASIC SKILLS AGENCY – INITIAL ASSESSMENT OF LITERACY AND NUMERACY

The desire to improve talent can start with even the very young. The Basic Skills Agency is an independent organization, working at 'arms length' from the English and Welsh governments. Its role is to improve 'the ability to read, write and speak in English/Welsh and to use mathematics at a level necessary to function and progress at work and in society in general'.

One of its outputs is the Initial Assessment of Literacy and Numeracy. It measures the basic literacy and numeracy of adults and young people over 16. The scores for each measure are converted into one of five attainment standards, as defined by the 'Adult Basic Skills Strategy Unit'. There are three versions of each test, versions one and two being for general use with post-16s, and version three for use in family learning programmes. The literacy tests cover basic spelling and grammar, the appropriate use of words, and simple reasoning and comprehension. The numeracy tests cover: simple addition, subtraction, multiplication, division; simple fractions and decimals; reading from a ruler and scale; telling the time using a timetable; working out area, perimeter and volume; interpreting scaling and reading from a graph.

So as with MOST above, even when recruiting school leavers into the organization, psychometric tests can assist an organization to get the best candidates available.

POSITIONING IN 360-DEGREE ASSESSMENT

Figure 3.1 below refers to the relationship between attitude, skill and knowledge within the context of integrated assessment. At this stage, we are looking at behavioural characteristics, that is, attitude, but this relationship will be referred to again in Chapter 4 (Figure 4.1) under the heading of Knowledge Assessment.

Clearly all the types of psychometric test can be applied in a 360-degree assessment, whether at the recruitment stage or for developmental purposes.

Aptitude tests which measure the differences in ability to perform or carry out different tasks are commonly used. These will normally centre around verbal or numerical reasoning. The results can then be compared with those of people already employed in the sort of position being considered.

The same will then apply to the personality and attitude tests described in this Chapter – do the profiles match with those considered suitable for the tasks associated with the role?

Having the right 'personality' is of course only part of the picture. Whether or not the applicant has the right knowledge to do the job is also critical. If the post or promotion opportunity is for one of the professions then evidence of passing the exams of the relevant body will be required, together with confirmation that the person has availed themselves of the Continuing Professional Development opportunities associated with the qualification. For other types of role, where professional qualifications are not a pre-requisite, then some form of knowledge assessment (dealt with in Chapter 4) can be used.

Then, of course, there is the interview. This is where areas of concern which the psychometric tests and knowledge assessments have highlighted can be probed. It also allows the interviewer to assess the applicant's social skills. It

NAME	TITLE	ATTITUDE	SKILL	KNOWLEDGE	INTEGRATED
John Webster	Account Manager	4	4	2	32/125
Tony Blake	Sales Executive	1	4	4	16/125
Barry Lewis	New Sales Business	5	4	4	80/125

Figure 3.1   The position of attitude in integrated assessment

is also the area of greatest subjectivity. The interviewer's biases and prejudices can often lead to candidates for a job position or a promotion being treated either too generously or too harshly because of the particular interviewer. This fact alone is one of the main reasons for the growth in the use of psychometric tests and knowledge assessments.

DEVELOPING A PSYCHOMETRIC TEST

The two terms most often applied to the development of psychometric tests are that of validity and reliability.

Psychometric tests need to be both reliable, that is to say that whatever attributes they measure, they do so with accuracy and precision, and valid, which means that the test fulfils its objectives by measuring what it purports to measure.

The term 'standardized' will also often be applied to psychometric tests, meaning that the tests have been used on a wide population sample against which subsequent respondents' results can be compared. It is this comparative measure that enables predictions to be made from the test results about a person's likely behaviour in different situations, for example in a new employment position.

It is therefore necessary that a psychometric test must undergo extensive and complete trials during its development. For example, a new psychometric test, cdaq, which is based on cognitive psychology and neurolinguistic programming (NLP), underwent four years of rigorous empirical testing before applying for accreditation by the British Psychological Society. The authors, cda, the UK-based organizational development and change management consultancy, involved a wide range of private and public sector organizations in its validation process, including Toyota GB, the Alpha Airports Group, Northern Foods and Essex County Council. Note also the 16PF5 questionnaire referred to above, where 2500 people were used for normative purposes in the USA and over 1300 in the UK.

WHAT EXACTLY DOES RELIABILITY MEAN?

Reliability is a measure of a test's ability to produce consistent results. What this means is that if the person were to take the test on several different occasions then they would obtain the same result. There may of course be 'practice effects', which means that if a person takes an aptitude test several times, they are likely to improve their score each time simply due to the effect of practice. However, when assessing the reliability of a test, psychologists are able to use statistical techniques to control this effect.

Reliability is normally expressed in terms of an index called the reliability coefficient. This index ranges from 0 to 1, with 0 meaning no reliability whatsoever and 1 meaning 100 per cent reliability. The reliability of a good aptitude test is normally somewhere between 0.8 and 0.9. The reliability of a personality test coefficient tends to be lower for a variety of reasons, but would normally be 0.7 or above. The test publishers will normally indicate the reliability coefficients in the test manual.

Reliability is considered to be an essential characteristic of any test. If a test cannot measure something consistently, then it cannot be the basis for valid inferences being drawn about the person being assessed. However, reliability by itself is not enough to create a successful psychometric test. A test must also be valid for the purpose for which it is going to be used. Validity is in fact the most important consideration when evaluating a test.

WHAT EXACTLY DOES VALIDITY MEAN?

The term validity can be defined in two ways: (a) the ability of the test to assess what it is supposed to assess; and (b) the ability of the test to allow valid inferences to be drawn from its results.

Psychologists measure validity in different ways and refer to different types of validity. They will say that a psychometric test has 'construct validity' if indeed the test measures the psychological attribute (or construct) that it purports to measure. Thus, an intelligence test is said to be valid if it does indeed measure how much intelligence a person has. This is often difficult to prove, as it means you would have to have another, accurate measure of intelligence to compare it to.

For this reason, in talent management situations (particularly selection) a second form of validity, 'predictive validity', is more relevant. Predictive validity is the ability of a test or questionnaire to make specific predictions about something that can be objectively assessed. For example, if developing a psychometric test to assess 'sales potential', it could be validated by following up the sample group of sales personnel who had been given the questionnaire in the trial period, to see if those who got high scores on the 'sales potential' dimension really did have higher sales figures a year later than those who got low scores. Therefore as with reliability, validity is an essential characteristic of a test.

HOW IS A PSYCHOMETRIC TEST DEVISED?

The first stage in developing a test is to undertake research into the area of aptitude or personality that is to be assessed by the test. In the case of an aptitude test, this would involve researching the components that make up the aptitude in question and the way the aptitude is demonstrated in the performance of tasks. This will lead to the sorts of questions or exercises that will be able to assess that ability. The case of personality is more complex and involves looking into the nature of personality and how it is structured in terms of particular dimensions.

Personality questionnaires are normally based on a particular 'model' of personality. There are many different models of personality, each of which offers a different perspective upon human behaviour, and each of which leads to a quite different set of questions or exercises when developing a personality test.

Once the initial research stage has been completed, the next stage involves writing trial test items, questions and exercises, and testing these out on samples of people. The purpose of this alpha testing stage is to see if the items work in practice, whether the questions can be understood, whether they are reliable, and whether each item appears to be assessing the ability or dimension of personality it is supposed to assess. This stage of the process can be long, involving several iterations of writing and rewriting questions and testing them out in practice. It is at this stage that any ambiguity in the questions is removed.

The next stage is to assemble the best items from the initial alpha trial stages into something that will correspond to the final test. This beta test is once again trialled and the data from the trial is used to construct the final version.

The last stage is called 'standardization'. This is where the final version of the test is administered to a large sample of people, normally called the 'standardization sample', which is representative of the sort of people the test will be used on in the future. The sample would include at least several hundred people and often significantly more than this. The data acquired during this stage are used to construct the norm tables that will later be used to convert the raw scores obtained from the test into 'standardized scores'. These standardized scores express an individual's test result in terms of a comparison with the performance of the people in the standardization sample. It is the accuracy of this procedure that will give the predictive validity referred to in the section above.

THE BENEFITS OF PSYCHOMETRIC TESTS IN TALENT MANAGEMENT

The search for talent and its retention is one of the most critical issues facing an organization today. In this Chapter we have explored the types of psychometric tests and have seen how they fit into the wider area of assessment.

Properly developed and valid psychometric tests have established their place in the professional organization's kit bag.

The benefits of using them can be summarized as follows:

- They are objective. There is no possibility of interviewer bias or prejudice based on age, sex, religion or politics.

- They are consistent. All candidates get the same questions or exercises in the same order and are allowed the same time to answer them, assuming the psychometric tests are taken in a controlled environment in line with the author's guidelines. There are now variations on this where some online verbal and numerical reasoning tests create a unique set of questions from a large bank of questions, where each question is deemed to be of equal difficulty, thereby still allowing comparative scoring.

- They are effective predictors of performance. Many studies show that the use of a quality psychometric test in conjunction with knowledge assessments and structured interviewing increases the effectiveness of recruitment.

- They offer 'self awareness' insights to the candidate as well as the organization. The feeling that an individual is learning and developing personally is an important motivator and, therefore, retention agent.

- They improve team effectiveness by allowing the team members to understand their own preferences and work styles as well as understanding those of their team colleagues.

- They are cost effective. As the market now has many different psychometric tests, the majority of which are available online, the costs associated with them are now very reasonable.

So we have established that psychometric tests are an invaluable tool for talent management. They are particularly useful in the following areas:

- recruitment

- career development

- personal development

- profiling and benchmarking existing exemplars to assist in future selection exercises

- succession planning

- team building.

CASE STUDIES: PUTTING PSYCHOMETRIC TESTS TO WORK

CASE STUDY 1: GRADUATE RECRUITMENT

The situation

How do you ensure you recruit the best talent into your company? Well, one of the UK's fastest growing business advisory firms decided that you should start with the graduate intake. It was already using a paper-based psychometric test to assist with this, where the candidates used to come in to the office in which they would be working if successful, take the test and be interviewed by some of the managerial staff. However, as the company was currently hiring almost 1000 graduates a year this process was becoming very time consuming and costly. It was also inconvenient for the candidates.

Key issues

The company wanted to reduce the effort and money it spent in the recruitment of graduates while at the same time easing the application burden on the candidates, who currently had to spend time travelling to the appropriate office, sit the test and be interviewed, with only a one in ten chance of success. If it could do this, as well as saving money, the reduced effort for would-be applicants would also be a positive selling point to future graduate applicants.

Problems to overcome

The previous test had been useful but the company decided it needed a fresh approach. It wanted a test that would have a higher correlation with success in the careers that the graduates were applying for, something that could be undertaken by the applicants in their own home yet would still give an accurate reading of their abilities.

Managers at the various offices were spending many thousands of hours interviewing candidates who had little or no chance of being offered a job. This often became apparent at the start of the interview, but out of politeness most of the managers persevered with the full interview; wasting more time than was necessary and creating a false expectation in the mind of the applicants.

The solution

The company approached one of the leading psychometric test providers and outlined the situation. The test provider devised a new test that covered both verbal and numerical reasoning. This was devised to reflect the competencies that would be required in the chosen career path. As the test would be taken online by the candidates, without any supervision, each individual test comprised random questions from a large bank of questions, each of equal difficulty, so that the risks of having a prior knowledge of the content would be minimal. The fact that each question had equal difficulty meant that two candidates could be objectively and fairly compared even if they did not actually have to answer any of the same questions.

Outcome and benefits achieved

The first benefit has been a dramatic reduction in managerial overheads associated with interviewing the applicants. This is reckoned to run to many thousands of hours. There is also a significant reduction in the expenses paid out for interview attendance.

The test results on average weed out about 60 per cent of applicants, meaning that those who do come for interview now have a one in four chance of success. In addition, the management experience of interviewing is much more pleasant as the managers know that each applicant has already demonstrated superior performance and will be worth interviewing.

This modern process to graduate recruitment also saves the applicant time and effort and this is used to promote the company to aspiring applicants as part of the university promotion exercises.

Although the company is undertaking more research, early results from the tests show a high correlation between the scores gained in the online verbal and numerical tests and performance in the professional exams subsequently taken.

Reinforcement programme

The adoption of the online testing has allowed graduates to apply for positions throughout the year. In addition, the company has set minimum degree and A-level standards, and so only graduates who pass these levels are invited to take the online test. This also means that the numbers of graduates needed to be interviewed for each post is falling and is now at one in three. This all helps the company stay ahead by recruiting the best young talent in a modern, streamlined and effective way.

CASE STUDY 2: SUCCESSION PLANNING

The situation

One of the world's fastest growing computer companies became concerned that it had not invested enough effort into succession planning and as a result did not know if individuals coming through the organization had the right skills to take up senior management positions. This was particularly important as the fast growth it had experienced meant that there was increasing demand for more senior managers. If there was a dearth of appropriately talented managers then it would need to embark on a significant recruitment exercise, and while this might provide the management capability, the recruits would be lacking in relevant company experience.

Key issues

It was important as a first step to identify what competencies actually affected performance. The company hired a consultancy familiar with psychometric tests to undertake this analysis. Although the company had been using over 30 competencies in a loosely applied way up to that point, after research the consultants identified ten competencies that did materially affect performance and indicated that three of them seemed to be really important. The critical ones were: tenacity, resilience and motivation.

Problems to overcome

As with many large organizations, promotion to first-line manager had been based on how good the managers were at their previous specialist roles, be it sales, marketing, engineering or software development. No real thought had been put into what competencies were needed for these first-line managerial positions. This discrepancy between competencies held as opposed to competencies necessary to do the job in hand would become even more important when looking at second-line managerial posts. There was also the problem associated with highly important jobs such as major account managers, crucial to the growth of the company and requiring yet another set of competencies to that of second-line managers.

The solution

The solution was provided by a leading provider of psychometric tests, who designed a two-day 'assessment centre', which considered the different competencies associated with the jobs described above.

The assessment included group exercises, verbal and numerical reasoning and the OPQ personality measures (referred to earlier in this Chapter). Output from this would give insight into the three critical areas of tenacity, resilience and motivation. The verbal and numerical reasoning gave indications of intellectual capability, while the group exercises allowed both team roles and leadership skills to be assessed.

Each attendee was then given face-to-face feedback and received a written report which said how well they had done on the competencies relevant for their next position. Each attendee then set up an interview with their line manager to agree development activities necessary to reach the right level for any competency that fell below the requisite level. As this exercise was conducted independently from any senior job appointments, even those candidates who needed significant development in a number of competency areas did not feel that they had lost out but rather that they were being given a significant opportunity to improve and develop.

Outcome and benefits achieved

The assessment centres were a great success, with all individuals finding the feedback both useful and motivational. As a result of this investment in them by the company, and as a result of the subsequent competency improvement training, there was an unexpected benefit to the company, in that staff turnover rates also fell.

From the company's point of view it was also able to put succession plans in place that had a much longer implementation phase. These included the development programme linking the future level of competencies required for the senior positions with the employees' existing levels, and a plan to bridge the gaps.

There were areas where the company realized it did not have talented middle managers coming up through the organization. It tackled this by recruiting them from outside at middle management level, so by the time they were ready for the senior positions they would also have had experience working with the company, and be familiar with its policies, procedures and politics.

Reinforcement programme

The company is now aligning its key competencies across the world and is adopting the assessment centre approach to recruitment. This ensures that the middle managers being recruited really are the most talented.

It also now holds internal succession planning events on a regular basis, giving individuals the chance to match their personal development in line with their planned career progression.

CASE STUDY 3: CREATION OF A DIVISIONAL BOARD OF A MULTINATIONAL FTSE 100 COMPANY

The situation

A major UK-based multinational FTSE 100 company had been growing rapidly by acquisition. Amongst its portfolio it had acquired eight IT companies that together represented a turnover of some £500 million. It decided that these would be more successful if they operated as one division within the group. This, they felt, would provide a greater market presence, economies of scale, cross-selling opportunities as well as cost savings through shared support services.

Key issues

Each of the eight smaller companies had its own operating board, often headed by the individuals who had founded the companies and developed them into successful organizations that had become attractive enough for the FTSE company to buy them. These boards so far had been allowed to operate autonomously within the group, reporting back primarily on financial performance.

Problems to overcome

Each individual board had been developed over a number of years and the quality of the directors varied enormously. However, each of the Managing Directors was fiercely protective of their own team, putting each one forward as top calibre. Not surprisingly, each Managing Director thought that they should become the new CEO of the larger organization.

Each company also operated its own policies and procedures which did not always comply with those suggested by the group functions, such as HR, IT, Finance and Marketing.

Therefore Group HR considered that a traditional interview process, supported by endorsements from the eight MDs, would not identify the best candidates. This was compounded by the fact that the sizes of the eight companies varied considerably and the board of directors of the larger two companies felt that they were the natural candidates for the new divisional roles.

The solution

The Group HR department, working with a variety of external consultants, decided to create a management assessment programme that would last for a six-month period. Each of the functional heads, such as finance directors, marketing directors and so on, attended specific assessment days that analysed their 'function specific' competencies. This included knowledge assessments even for those with professional qualifications, as these had often been obtained many years previously and not all the directors had been keeping as up to date as they might have.

There was also a series of multi-disciplinary events with attendees taken from different operating companies where exercises were devised to assess how individuals operated in a team. This included: team preference roles, based on the work of Meredith Belbin referred to above, and exercises designed to show degrees of assertiveness, empathy and leadership. While stopping short of outward-bound exercises, the events did include a variety of 'management games' which required effective teamwork and where the teams would not do well unless the members demonstrated strong leadership, delegation and creative-thinking skills.

Finally, Group HR developed a shortlist of candidates for the top Divisional Director positions – on average three for each job – and these each attended a full day with an occupational psychologist where they undertook verbal and numerical reasoning tests as well as structured interviews that explored their motivations and aspirations.

The attendees were then given face-to-face feedback and a written report to aid their personal and professional development in the future.

Outcome and benefits achieved

The Group appointed the divisional board of directors and the new CEO in the full knowledge that they had selected the most appropriate candidates rather than taking the subjective views of any of the existing MDs. In turn the aspiring directors also appreciated how thorough the process had been and the unsuccessful candidates received valuable feedback regarding their abilities and motivations.

A number of the unsuccessful candidates did leave the organization as a result but went to roles that they felt were more appropriate for them based on their newly increased self-awareness. Many of the others stayed on as senior managers and again based on the feedback they had received in the assessment process were able to agree development plans that would make them more likely to gain the top job next time.

An unexpected benefit was that three of these senior managers actually stayed with the Group but switched disciplines to ones more suited to their competencies and motivation. This benefited the individuals and meant that the company also retained their invaluable knowledge and experience of company products, services and markets.

Reinforcement programme

Group HR considered the exercise to have been a major success and has continued with many parts of the programme, using it for external recruitment, management promotion boards and succession planning events. It has succeeded in developing the concept that promotion is gained on merit and not on the basis of 'who you know'.

CHAPTER 4

Elements of Knowledge Assessment

INTRODUCTION

Knowledge assessment, or KA, is a process by which the knowledge base of a business practitioner, in commerce, industry or the professions, can be measured to determine how well they know what to do and when to do it, in order to generate progress towards the achievement of assigned objectives.

In other words, it is not a measurement of behavioural issues, such as determination to succeed or being available to solve problems but more a matter of ensuring that capability with regard to providing the correct information is maintained at precisely the right level, for example, to both customers and internal senior management.

HOW DID THE NEED FOR KNOWLEDGE ASSESSMENT ARISE?

Traditionally, people have attended training and development courses to improve or enhance their effectiveness. How was the suitability of the course determined? Content? Level? Relevance? Whatever the case, one thing can be certain – few general courses or workshops would be appropriate for individual requirements.

Typically, a person who attended a three-day workshop on, say, sales management, would come away saying, 'Monday was quite good – I learnt a few good tips. Tuesday, I thought, was a complete waste of time – I don't need to know about exponential smoothing for inventory management. Wednesday, OK, the session on sales forecasting was good, in line with the previous day's session but we don't do forecasting in our company in this way'.

So why send someone on a training course where perhaps only 30 per cent of the content is really relevant?

This is where knowledge assessment comes in.

HOW DOES KNOWLEDGE ASSESSMENT WORK?

The first thing to be considered is how it is constructed, particularly since it is a relatively recent development and must gain the approval of HR professionals who will need to know how it is validated prior to release as a useable service.

First of all it measures knowledge that will ultimately lead to skill enhancement. It is based upon a recognized body of knowledge, the mechanics of which will be covered later in this Chapter. It primarily deals with those elements that enable the practitioner to know, at all times, what to do next. For example, imagine a salesperson who has completed the initial qualification of a prospective client. That is to say, the level of contact is correct, there is a real need and the client has set aside (maybe as a result of the salesperson's encouragement) a budget dedicated to the procurement of the new project in question. Good news! What does the salesperson do next or how is the sale progressed?

There may be a number of options:

- decide to bid for the business unconditionally;
- bring in a manager to verify the quality of the situation;
- carry out a survey of customer requirements in detail;
- arrange reference site visits;
- make a presentation to the people responsible for the decision.

Whatever the salesperson decides to do is classified as option selling, but the key issue is 'Does the salesperson know what to do?'

This is one of the many aspects of knowledge assessment. We are not so much concerned with behavioural tendencies (although there could be some overlap) as much as pure knowledge of the process.

WHO USES KNOWLEDGE ASSESSMENT?

Unlike some other forms of assessment, individuals who wish to 'test out' their capability do not necessarily gear it for personal use. Typically, large enterprises will use it to assess the quality of their business practitioners over a planned period.

First of all, selected people will be assessed for a number of different reasons:

- selection and recruitment

- training needs analysis

- identification of candidates in line for promotion

- recognizing top performer characteristics

- optimizing the workforce.

An immediate application emerges in the area of talent management where all of the above can be consolidated to recognize the very best candidates, from a knowledge viewpoint, to be the future strength of the company.

Experience has shown that line management, anxious to assess their direct reports, have used knowledge assessment, particularly where a newly-appointed manager needs to review the people that have been 'inherited'. HR, generally, are involved in the use of knowledge assessment where comprehensive assessment of existing and future hires is needed. In this case, HR professionals, familiar with its capability, will incorporate knowledge measurement as part of the overall assessment process.

Towards the end of this Chapter, specific illustrations of the applications of knowledge assessment will be given.

POSITIONING OF KNOWLEDGE ASSESSMENT IN 360-DEGREE ASSESSMENT

The three major areas of assessing a suitable candidate for employment, promotion or fast-tracking for talent management purposes are based upon the generally accepted relationship: ASK – Attitude, Skill, Knowledge.

All three can be measured individually and then illustrated to provide a very accurate overall assessment.

If we measure knowledge together with attitude and skill, we can come up with a level of capability which for comparative purposes focuses on the overall effectiveness for future development.

For example, let us assume that we rate a salesperson on a scale of 1–5 in each of the three sections, where 5 equals excellent, 4 very good, 3 good, 2 above average, 1 average, illustrating a maximum score of 125 if we multiply all factors together. If we were to apply the formula for integrated assessment we might come up with the following equation in the examples given in Figure 4.1.

Therefore, it can be concluded that if attitude is apparently high and skill is at a similar level, but knowledge is low, effectiveness is limited. By the same token, if attitude is low but skill and knowledge are high the net result still presents a problem. In the third example, where all three factors are recognized to be at a high level the real measurement is significant.

As far as knowledge assessment is concerned the grades are: 5 = excellent (75 per cent+); 4 = very good (66–74 per cent); 3 = good (60–65 per cent); 2 = above average (55–59 per cent); 1 = average (50–54 per cent). If we could apply a similar measurement to the attitude and skill factors we are in a position to make a meaningful across-the-board comparison.

It is important to remember that KA measures knowledge rather than any other factor. Therefore, if a candidate scores badly on KA, it does not necessarily mean that all is lost; it generally indicates that knowledge enhancement by specific training areas is required. By the same token, a high score in KA does not suggest a clear and free path to success. All three factors of ASK need to be at a high level before we can start thinking about serious personal development programmes for key personnel.

KA STRUCTURES

THE BODY OF KNOWLEDGE

The basis upon which a KA is formulated is generally described as a body of knowledge. The following illustrates a summary of a typical body of knowledge for a general management assessment.

NAME	TITLE	ATTITUDE	SKILL	KNOWLEDGE	INTEGRATED
John Webster	Account Manager	4	4	2	32/125
Tony Blake	Sales Executive	1	4	4	16/125
Barry Lewis	New Sales Business	5	4	4	80/125

Figure 4.1   Integrated assessment

SCOPE

1. *Decision-making criteria*: A close examination of decision-making processes, the qualities required to be a sound decision-maker, the correct use of concurrence from support staff, the effect of decision-making and consequences of both positive and negative effects.

2. *Delegation*: The way in which delegation is planned, the doctrine of completed staff work, staff and line organizations, the structure of effective delegation and job enrichment as opposed to job enlargement.

3. *Motivation and leadership*: A comprehensive subject covering a number of key issues such as characteristics of a healthy organization, the dangers of organizational stagnation, establishment of favourable working conditions, the types of power in an organization, cross-company support and management functions versus management skills.

4. *Managing change*: Probably one of the most difficult subjects for newly-appointed managers to grasp but is essential as part of an organizational development process. The assessment questions in this section will cover change philosophy and the ways in which both managers and professionals can ensure the successful management and implementation of change. Most importantly, the questions will concentrate upon the need for reinforcement of the change process prior to operational handover.

5. *Teamwork*: A massive subject; but the concentration of focus is upon team productivity. In particular, the specific characteristics of an undeveloped team, that is to say, a group of possibly experienced people who may be working together for the first time. Other questions will need to address how to manage different people from different standpoints, for example, how to bring in loners, pessimists, non-conformists and over-optimists into the team to ensure effective working and unity. This section also covers the management of conflict, both healthy and unhealthy.

6. *Appraisal, counselling and coaching*: Again, a broad subject. One that concentrates upon goals and objective setting with emphasis upon the need to set realistic targets, involving the subordinate's 'buy in' to the processes involved. As part of formal appraisal systems, meaningful goals are integrated into the appraisal process and guidelines are provided for the ways in which appraisal and

counselling interviews should be conducted. Questions in this area should also move into factors involved in assessing people for promotion coupled with the ways in which feedback to a higher management potential programme can be structured.

7.   *Time management*: Generally represents something of a blockage for both new and recently appointed managers (1–2 years' experience). One of the major reasons is due to the difficulty in relinquishing technical capability for true management function. The section deals with good time management practices and contrasts those functions that are often regarded by more experienced people as 'confusing activity with achievement'. The theme throughout this module is based upon the transition from professional to managerial responsibility in terms of time management.

8.   *Communication*: This section deals with the various types of communication and the effects of media distortion. It also involves the ways in which complexities of channels can affect both verbal and written communication. Considerable emphasis is placed upon how 'difficult' people can best be managed in terms of the ways in which communication can become most effective. Several elements of interpersonal communication are covered and there is emphasis upon the provision of guidelines for handling the communication 'politics' of an organization. In simple terms, it provides a short-circuit for the ways in which inexperienced (and not so inexperienced) managers should conduct themselves in a corporate environment.

9.   *Selection and recruitment*: Identifies the ways in which the total selection process is best covered, from the need to provide additional headcount, through job descriptions, into the initial elements of selection, normally involving an HR function. It provides a clear structure for conducting interviews at various levels and amassing sufficient information to reach a balanced recruitment decision.

10. *Finance*: Essentially 'finance for non-financial management'. It provides a basic insight into budgetary control, cost control and financial planning. It does not extend into some of the more complex processes of specialist financial management but provides any manager who needs to understand basic financial processes, with the likely procedures any company is liable to take.

11.   *Negotiation*: The emphasis is upon the personal qualities required to become an effective negotiator and this is then followed up by the various negotiation platforms, for example team or solo negotiations. It also covers the perception of the 'buyer' and how to prepare effectively for different types of negotiation processes. In particular, the focus is upon the true effects of practical negotiation and some of the hidden dangers if too much is given away too soon.

This is the scaffolding of the KA from which the questionnaire can be built. The most important thing to bear in mind about a body of knowledge is that it has to represent, very closely, all the competencies that a practitioner in business will need to know in order to do the job effectively.

A number of professional bodies such as the Association for Project Management (APM) in the UK and the Project Management Institute (PMI) in the USA have comprehensive and established bodies of knowledge as do some engineering institutes.

QUESTIONNAIRE DEVELOPMENT

The following is an outline of the structure of a typical general management assessment.

50 questions cover management issues and the categories covered fall into 11 distinct sections:

- decision-making criteria
- delegation
- motivation and leadership
- managing change
- teamwork
- appraisal and counselling
- time management
- communication
- selection and recruitment
- finance
- negotiation skill.

The assessment has been designed to take a *snapshot* of knowledge in those sections mentioned above.

There is also a pre-assessment process in which the above sections have explanations of the content of each. Grids are provided to enable the participant to self-assess on a scale of up to 10, the importance and also, the individual's perceived knowledge level for each section. This self-assessment will be taken into account in arriving at the final evaluation. There is a finite amount of time in which the assessment should be completed.

Some questions are marked 'You may select only one' and others 'you may select more than one'. There are also some questions that require the answer to be put into a numerical sequence.

The following are examples of the type of questions contained in a typical assessment.

EXAMPLE 1

Which of the following describes a sound decision-maker?

You may select only one.

    a)   Thinks things through; makes a decision alone and announces it promptly to subordinates.

    b)   Seeks consensus but makes own decision.

    c)   Makes decisions mostly by gaining agreement from the 'committee'.

    d)   Delegates the decision to those who will be held accountable.

    e)   Only acts on advice from the 'invisible decision-maker'.

EXAMPLE 2

Which of the following conditions can result in organization stagnation?

You may select more than one.

    a)   Inadequate training.

    b)   Unrealistically high payment packages.

    c)   Top management getting close to the workforce.

    d)   Constantly changing mission statement.

e)   Task-orientated management approach.

EXAMPLE 3

Which of the following actions relating to references do you believe will be of use in checking a candidate's claims?

You may select more than one.

a)   Request two work-related and one general reference.

b)   Seek a reference from an established credit agency.

c)   Investigate the existence of a criminal record.

d)   Ask whether the previous employer would re-hire when taking up verbal references.

MARKING ALGORITHMS

The key to accuracy, reliability of results and integrity of KA is the marking: using the + 0 – (plus, zero, minus) convention is generally used to best effect.

In practice, this means that any option within the multi-choice questionnaire attracts plus points for a correct selection, zero if the selection makes no difference and minus points if the selection does not match the 'hoped-for' response. All this gives us a real insight to the knowledge base of the participant.

At the micro level, we can see that certain aspects of, say, delegation may be correct or in need of improvement.

At the macro level, in combination with other interpersonal factors, we may see that people-handling skills may either be good or the candidate may have a shortfall of knowledge requiring immediate attention.

Let's look at a specific example:

Take the following question:

With which of the following statements do you agree?

a)   You can delegate to the person with the least work to do.

b)   Effective delegation assists in the development of subordinates.

c)   If your manager calls you in to discipline you for the mistake of one of your people to whom you delegated a task, you protest strongly that the fault is not yours.

d)   Once you have signed a document prepared by your subordinate for your signature, it is no longer the subordinate's responsibility.

e)   Delegation means that the subordinate is working with the authority of the manager.

In this case, the participant has selected options b), d) and e) which might all attract positive points. Option a) could well be zero and c) minus.

This, however, is by no means the end of the story regarding the total scope of the marking algorithm. The assessment needs to be normalized so that it is set at a notional 'pass' level. This is generally 50 per cent or the average level. The skill in developing an accurate KA lies in formulating the marking algorithm to produce a true assessment for the average performer at the normalization levels. Below this level is described simply as below average.

As mentioned earlier in this chapter under ASK, subsequent levels are: above average; good; very good; excellent.

The mix of level results based upon a sample of 100 candidates taking the same assessment at the same time, at the same job level, with similar experience, in the same industry, for comparison purposes typically is:

Below average	11
Average	47
Above average	26
Good	14
Excellent	2

This now begins to show some interesting statistics around the knowledge base of similar people. For a start, only 2 per cent of people display an outstanding level of knowledge. A further 14 per cent need 'fine-tuning' as far as their knowledge is concerned and if we were to draw a line under the Average performers, or those likely to perpetuate mediocrity unless some development is undertaken, only 42 per cent of people are 'on top of things' as far as knowing what to do and when to do it is concerned. Less than half the sample!

Since the advent of KA, regular users of the process have seen that it provides the missing link of 360-degree assessment. Without KA, there is a considerable risk of hiring the wrong person or promoting a person to an assignment beyond their capability.

Getting the marking algorithm absolutely right provides an exceptional level of accuracy, allowing KA to be completely relied upon as input to a balanced assessment process.

PROTOTYPE TESTING

Once the basic questionnaire is written and the marking algorithm has been formulated, there now comes three phases of testing to ensure that the KA product does the job. This vital validation process must take place before any assessment can be considered viable and therefore effective in the field. This can take months or even a year or two to satisfy all the conditions needed to represent a fair assessment of someone's knowledge.

1. ALPHA-TESTING

Ideally as many participants as possible should be invited to act as volunteers to take the assessment under controlled conditions. In practice, at least one hundred participants of varying knowledge/experience are selected. The results are compiled and the KA developer looks for patterns in correct and incorrect responses to the options in the questionnaire. Clear anomalies such as ambiguity of meaning and specialist terminology come under close scrutiny. Interviews are carried out with selected participants who are also asked to complete an 'experience' report. This covers the reaction to the assessment and invites constructive comment for review. Any changes required at this stage are made and preparations are put in place for the second phase.

2. BETA-TESTING

At this time, different practitioners of, say, a minimum of five years' experience in the discipline are invited to participate. The size of the group may be smaller, say, 50, but every effort is made to ensure that a degree of homogeneity of likely knowledge/experience is available. Again, the assessments are marked but this time based upon a clear removal of impediments of understanding. The participants are asked a series of questions, in addition to the 'experience' report, the most important of all being, 'Does this assessment, in your opinion, represent a fair run-down of the knowledge you require to do your job now, and in the foreseeable future?'

All responses are taken on board and opinions of the participants carefully filtered. Changes that are needed to be made are carried out and preparations are made for the final phase.

3. FIELD-TESTING

In this last part of the programme and prior to release of a product into the market, three or more target companies, experienced users of other current KA products, would be asked to provide a number of people to participate in the field-test with an important pre-requisite – the line managers of the assessment participants should acknowledge that they have a detailed understanding of their people's capability for comparison with the assessment results.

There are always some surprises when the evaluations are released!

Once this final phase is complete and all known issues resolved, the assessment is ready for use.

The serious limitations, however, are the number of tests that could be marked in a reasonable time frame and customization of the tests to match specific user requirements.

If a large enterprise such as a bank or a major Government department, where hundreds, if not thousands of practitioners, say project professionals, needed to be tested, the task would be almost impossible to complete in a time frame acceptable to the customer.

A better way of managing high volumes of tests, or now assessments, as the market prefers to call them, is urgently needed. This means only one thing: the assessments needed to be taken online via the Internet.

First of all, a comprehensive debriefing summary can be prepared, showing the precise areas where the participant's answers caused a difference between the expected answers and actual answers. This enables the line manager or supervisor of the participant to indicate why there was an apparent problem. For example, if a participant gets a low score in a particular category it is very easy to determine how that happened through a detailed examination of the questions involved.

Secondly, a comprehensive artificial intelligence system can be written to provide a detailed insight into the training requirements of the participant.

Thirdly, there are a number of methods by which automatic or manual debriefing processes can be provided. The online methods provide a thorough run-down of a participant's performance such that the interviewing manager can become an 'instant' counsellor, thus allaying any doubts or disappointments the participant may have.

PROVIDERS OF KNOWLEDGE ASSESSMENTS

There are a number of KA providers who concentrate upon knowledge measurement, rather than anything else, particularly in the field, for example, of project management.

Whereas traditionally managers may have relied upon 'gut feel' to assess a business practitioner, today there are organizations who have built KA-type products to provide a structured and standardized approach to this essential function. The following examples in project management were published in the monthly *Project Manager Today* in February 2006.

The PMI's basic knowledge assessment contains 150 multiple-choice questions. It is geared to their body of knowledge and takes three hours to complete and, when finished, summarizes the number of correct answers provided by the participant.

Then there is the APM Group's PCA (Project Management Capability Assessment). This is also a multi-choice questionnaire, developed jointly with SST International in booklet form in 1994, revised regularly, and now on the web.

Other organizations providing KAs in project management are PM Professional Learning with their knowledge assessment Tool (Knasto), The Projects Group's knowledge evaluation questionnaire, Provek's assessment tool designed to assist a participant in determining the best examination to take, and CITI's 24-question assessment designed to cover, in the space of 5–10 minutes, a participant's project management experience and the types of projects upon which experience has been gained.

Skillsedge provides, in addition to KAs on project management, other subjects such as sales, general management, business analysis and relationship management, all online.

OUTPUT FROM KNOWLEDGE ASSESSMENTS

Output from assessments includes evaluations, histograms, training needs analyses and debrief documentation.

EVALUATIONS

First of all, let us look at the following evaluation of a participant who has taken a general management capability assessment incorporating a sophisticated Artificial Intelligence (AI) system (see Figure 4.2).

The first thing to notice is that the evaluation starts with a summary, which highlights the key factors of the assessment. In this case, James has 'passed' six out of the eleven sections which represents the basis of determining any training priorities. Secondly, the categories James has cited as being of both High to Very High in terms of importance have been isolated as early training requirements if the assessment result is at variance with James's personal view. There then follows the detailed analysis of the areas where James's answers were different from the 'hoped-for' answers.

Then we come to the body of the assessment itself. Each of the eleven sections in this assessment contains a number of questions, all designed to take a 'snapshot' of a participant's knowledge in a specific competency. Again, where there is a difference, a comment is automatically generated by the AI system to provide the explanation as to why the issue has been highlighted. This needs to be reviewed for relevance to the current and any known future assignment. Sometimes it is the case that a particular section may be beyond the job description of the individual for the foreseeable future, for example finance for a first-line manager, but the question that needs to be addressed is whether this additional knowledge is desirable or likely to be essential as the process of managing the person's career in the future is concerned.

HISTOGRAMS

The power of a KA database enables the production of a wide variety of comparative histograms. From the above evaluation, we can compare James's performance with the rest of his company, GQ Electronics, and his positioning in the IT software services industry where he is a manager. As can be seen in Figure 4.3, the eleven sections of the general management assessment and James's overall rating can be easily measured to see how he measures up in the overall environment in which he operates.

GENERAL MANAGEMENT CAPABILITY ASSESSMENT

James Booth   Process Control Manager

GQ Electronics   Date of assessment: 29 June   Assessment No: 7894

Summary:

James has met or exceeded requirements in 6 of the 11 sections with an overall rating 4 percent above the norm for this assessment. With profiles of any level, there are always areas where improvement can be made and the detailed comments by section below, suggest some recommendations or tips that can be acted upon to improve management knowledge. Also, the training recommendations, as a result of comparing the self-assessment of the sections concerned and the actual scores, should be reviewed in terms of setting priorities for personal development and, again, are suggestions for improving longer-term requirements in accordance with training standards established by GQ Electronics.

The categories that have been self-assessed as being of High to Very High importance where the section score is less than the norm, suggest the possible training requirements. These are:

- Decision-making criteria
- Teamwork
- Communication
- Negotiation skill
- Finance.

However, it is important to check each of the categories cited above, for relevance to James's current or known future assignment. If necessary or desirable, the Competency Selection option for this assessment would give a clear indication of James's rating within the actual job definition now and in the future within the company, as well as the industry standards generally.

CATEGORY	SELF ASSESSMENT		% SCORE	PERCENTILE	TRAINING INDICATOR
	KNOWLEDGE	IMPORTANCE			
DECISION-MAKING CRITERIA	MEDIUM	HIGH	23	20	James does not appear to use a logical and sequential approach in formulating the ways in which sound decisions are made such that senior management may give approval for a major change. James would benefit from seeking feedback as to the effectiveness of decisions made, from everyone likely to be affected by such decisions. It is important to remember that accountability for decisions rests with the decision-maker. James may not be looking at all the alternatives and consequences with regard to making effective decisions.
DELEGATION	HIGH	VERY HIGH	85	100	Completed Staff Work is an extremely effective way of getting people to think through problems for themselves before presenting their manager with an unnecessary task. Making a realistic recommendation in handling a problem is far more worthwhile for everyone concerned. James seemed to be unfamiliar with this doctrine. James may need to understand more about the true role of line and staff management functions, if that is relevant to the organization.

Figure 4.2   **General management capability assessment**

CATEGORY	SELF ASSESSMENT		% SCORE	PERCENTILE	TRAINING INDICATOR
	KNOWLEDGE	IMPORTANCE			
MOTIVATION AND LEADERSHIP	MEDIUM	HIGH	56	65	James does not appear to recognize the key factors in helping people to become more effective in their assignments. James should guard against creating organization stagnation by actively encouraging training and people- as opposed to task-orientated management styles. James would benefit from a short workshop on Qualities required for Effective Leadership. The main characteristics of a healthy organization were not recognized in a key question on this important subject. Management motivation is more about controlling, monitoring, planning, organizing and co-ordinating rather than 'doing'. James seemed to be a little hazy about this.
MANAGING CHANGE	VERY HIGH	HIGH	67	100	James may not be constantly looking for better ways to manage the business and may be missing out on positive change opportunities.
TEAMWORK	VERY HIGH	VERY HIGH	27	40	James needs to be sensitive to the working patterns likely to be displayed by an undeveloped team to avoid the possibility of slowing down individual and team growth. If any of James's team members appear to be loners or do not 'conform', James should be very careful to ensure they are given every opportunity to feel part of the overall team effort. Again in the matter of Conflict Management, James should be more concerned with reaching agreement for future action rather than attempting just to apportion blame for the conflict caused.
COUNSELLING AND APPRAISAL	LOW	HIGH	68	85	James should review the ways in which goals and objectives are set and measured. It should be remembered that objectives set at individual level could well affect interfacing parties and this should be made clear at the time the objectives are agreed. James would benefit from paying particular attention to identifying resources required to achieve individual objectives, combined with monitoring procedures and reward mechanisms for achievement of objectives set. James does not appear to appreciate the true function of a formal appraisal system with particular regard to the amount of time involved in preparing thoroughly and the effect that an accurate appraisal can have upon Organization Development. James may not be looking at all the issues involved in assessing employees for promotion in an objective manner. Formal appraisal processes require that the documented support of the company precedes any interview. In other words, the employee, the manager and the superior manager need to be involved in a timely manner together with HR to ensure that standards are followed and that all documentation is properly approved before the interview process starts.

Figure 4.2　*Continued*

CATEGORY	SELF ASSESSMENT		% SCORE	PERCENTILE	TRAINING INDICATOR
	KNOWLEDGE	IMPORTANCE			
TIME MANAGEMENT	HIGH	HIGH	83	100	
COMMUNICATION	MEDIUM	HIGH	38	40	James needs to know more about the elements of effective communication in one-way and two-way communication, involving complexity of channels. James is likely to transcend the bounds of generally recognised good communication practice and this needs early review.
SELECTION AND RECRUITMENT	HIGH	MEDIUM	47	85	James should review the main issues for ensuring that a candidate to be interviewed for employment provides the correct basic information for example references, reasons for frequent job changes, and so on. It is important, when dealing with external specialists, to make certain that they have at least the hard and soft skill qualities equal to or better than internal candidates, before deciding to recruit. James omitted some key points in preparing for pre-interview checklists. James could certainly benefit from more insight into the ways in which an organization develops positive attributes for future development. For example, subject to recruitment policy, the company may seek to inject new blood into key management positions from outside the company, rather than just promote from within. Further, an environment in which training is regarded as an absolute necessity, rather than an interruption to routine, would engender the need to develop better people. These are both examples of recruitment practice supported by many leading companies in all fields of activity.
NEGOTIATION SKILL	HIGH	HIGH	43	45	Attendance at a Negotiations Skills workshop would be of value, as James does not seem to recognize all the personal qualities required of a successful negotiator. There is a marked difference between negotiating in teams rather than on an individual platform. James did not appear to appreciate the finer points of variance. The 'No-Concessions' type of negotiation needs further clarification, otherwise James will have a slight tendency to give too much away, too soon, for the wrong reasons.
FINANCE	MEDIUM	HIGH	14	0	If relevant to James's current assignment, or if the likelihood of becoming involved in Cost Control Processes is on the horizon in the foreseeable future, James needs some training in this specialist area.
OVERALL			54		

A percentile of 49, for example, shows that 48% of the people taking the assessment got a lower score.

Figure 4.2 *Continued*

There is virtually no limit to the coverage of meaningful histograms that can be produced, providing the necessary basic information is entered at the time the participant takes the assessment. A well-designed KA will cover:

- job type

- years of experience

- industry

- specialization

- personnel responsibility

- outline of known relevant strengths in the field of operation

- areas for improvement

- work location

- any other factors needed for meaningful comparison.

DEBRIEF INTERVIEWS

After the assessment is produced there is the option of a debrief interview between the assessment participant and the line manager or an external advisor. KA allows two types of debrief: manual collection of information from the answers provided in the booklet versions, or a fully automated debrief session, where the manager or advisor is given a comprehensive appraisal of all the questions in the assessment that were flagged for review. In the latter case, the manager or advisor is capable, with virtually no preparation, of demonstrating where the participant 'went wrong' and can discuss, from a position of strength, where priorities for future courses of corrective action may lie.

The interview can then be documented and provide input to the training needs analysis.

JAMES BOOTH – GQ ELECTRONICS – GENERAL MANAGEMENT ASSESSMENT HISTOGRAM

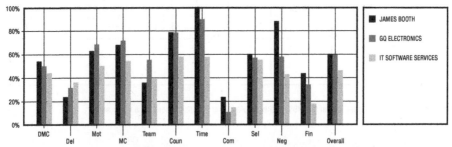

Figure 4.3   General management assessment histogram

TRAINING NEEDS ANALYSIS

This is the net distillation of exchange of information based upon discussion by the assessment participant and the person reviewing the results. It generally follows the pattern of extracting short-, medium- and long-term training needs in line with managing the person's progression through the company.

A typical training needs analysis (TNA) composed from the output from a general management assessment of and interviews with three participants is shown in Figure 4.4.

These would, in this case, represent the short-term training needs of three participants and would be further augmented by further TNAs as time progressed.

We now come on to a vital factor in assessment and training as part of any talent management programme using KA techniques.

One of the most difficult things to achieve in training is to ensure that the trainee retains the trained information. This is where KA can help. As we have seen, the participant sits the assessment to define training needs but is also informed that, say, six months after the training has been completed, the assessment will be taken again, a) to determine the effectiveness of the training and b) to ensure that the knowledge gained is still in place. This has an interesting effect; the participant does not just see a one-off assessment followed by a training course but a six-month period of continuing assessment during which time all the good things that have been learned have to be put into practice and retained for long-term use.

APPLICATIONS OF KA

Training needs analysis

A number of organizations have used knowledge assessment for determining the training needs of salespeople, project managers and general managers, business analysts and relationship managers.

Notably, organizations within the financial services sector have used the assessments for testing the quality of their sales forces. Banks use project management assessments to determine training requirements for a wide range of project professionals from project team leader right up to programme manager. Other organizations in many diverse industries have used and continue to

TRAINING NEEDS ANALYSIS

	JAMES BOOTH	BEATRICE PRICE	MICHAEL WRIGHT
DECISION MAKING CRITERIA			
TEAM BUILDING			
TIME MANAGEMENT			
COMMUNICATION SKILL			
SELECTION AND RECRUITMENT			
NEGOTIATION SKILL			
FINANCE			
DELEGATION			

Figure 4.4   Training needs analysis

use knowledge assessment for regular updating of training requirements for their business professionals. In particular, major enterprises use general management assessments to determine the quality level of their first- and second-line managers and provide training courses as a direct function of the assessment results.

Selection and recruitment

Virtually all users of KA use the process for facilitating recruitment decision-making for shortlisted candidates. In the case or salespeople, the cost of making the wrong decision can be very high; not only are recruitment costs wasted together with the salary while the person is employed, the opportunity cost in a sales territory that has not materialized can be very high. Many large organizations are staunch supporters of KA for sales recruits. In the case of project management, a number of departments in the public sector have clearly stated that the quality of their project teams is improving significantly by using KA to select the right people.

Determining effectiveness of training

As was mentioned above, the process normally consists of taking an assessment to design training courses and, say, six months after the training has been completed, sitting the assessment again to see whether the trained knowledge has been retained – one of the most difficult things to do in providing realistic training effectiveness. It is worth re-emphasizing this. By using KA with a pre-determined return date, the participant clearly understands that the training course following the assessment is not the end of the matter but will be measured again so that greater effort is made in applying the techniques covered in the training course. Examples of companies who have adopted this approach can be found where comprehensive internal training departments are established.

Managing talent or determining 'best of breed'

The situation occurs quite often where companies wish that they could attract more top performers rather than exist with just a mix of top and average people. By profiling their best performers, companies can recruit against such profiles, or as near as possible, to ensure that the knowledge and capability that they will attract will be of the right standard. There is always, of course, the question of how well the individual will fit into the company but that is better measured using psychometric methods to ensure that attitude and motivation are correct.

Downsizing

Unfortunately, due to economic requirements, redundancies in an organization have to be made. The question always is which current employees should be released. Some major enterprises have used KA to determine which employees' release would result in least risk to the business. In some large-scale redundancies, this can become a very expensive operation in the long run, if the wrong people leave the company resulting in a massive knowledge gap. Therefore careful assessment of all the people concerned is of paramount importance.

Acquisitions

Within the IT industry today and indeed many other industries, growth by acquisition is a common occurrence. All the processes of due diligence that need to be undertaken and warranties provided are, of course, part of the journey that needs to be made by both sides in order to ensure that what is being bought and sold represents the true situation. However, until the advent of KA, it might have been difficult to determine the quality of professional employees within an organization prior to finalizing a bid for the company in question. This is particularly important in a sales-oriented company where the quality of the sales force will be paramount in determining the effectiveness of the acquisition. By using KA, the bidding company will be able to determine very accurately, for example, the quality of the sales force they will be inheriting. The same could well apply to project managers and indeed the general management structure of the organization to be acquired.

SUMMARY OF THE EVOLUTION AND BENEFITS OF KNOWLEDGE ASSESSMENT

The need for knowledge assessment (KA) arose in the early 1990s when external training providers ran training events of a somewhat general nature even if they were customized to a specific industry or discipline. The main reason for this was, although the trainers would have taken great pains to understand the business objectives of their clients in terms of designing a training programme for a group of salespeople or managers, it was extremely difficult to cater for the knowledge levels of the individuals within the group, hence the problem that created the need to understand specific individual requirements prior to attendance on a training course.

Traditionally, most assessments of individual capability would have been based upon some form of behavioural testing, which was covered in detail in Chapter 3, but with the advent of KA, a new dimension, or missing link, could be provided to help reduce the risk of hiring or promoting the wrong person.

We therefore reach a point where it is important to understand that KA only represents one-third of a full 360-degree assessment. Indeed, all three methods of assessment (Attitude, Skill, Knowledge) contribute a similar percentage.

As KA is a relatively new assessment process, users should try to remember that a bad score in KA does not represent disaster; it means that with the appropriate development programme, in conjunction with support from the remaining assessments, a corrective course of action can be taken to put things right.

By the same token, a good score in KA does not necessarily mean that the participant will be successful. Much depends upon the balance of the other assessment elements, that is Attitude and Skill.

Figure 4.5 illustrates the effect of integrated or 360-degree assessment.

In an ideal environment, anyone can be heroic, but when there are difficult economic conditions or lowering demand for a product or service offering only those people with the necessary skills based upon a solid knowledge base are likely to continue to be successful.

Therefore, the authority of KA lies in its unquestioned worth and track record of achievement in providing the information necessary to identify those people who can excel under a wide range of conditions – those who have real talent and are being nurtured accordingly. The involvement of HR in this aspect of assessment and development is vital to the future success of any talent management programme (see Chapter 8, 'The Operational Role of HR').

We now come to the specific benefits of KA.

FOR THE PARTICIPANT

The benefits of KA for the participant are as follows:

- The ability to match self-assessment against proven measurement instruments in a very short period of time.

- Suspected shortfalls in knowledge can be confronted and corrected.

- Short-, medium- and long-term training programmes can be generated.

- Determining effectiveness of training is easy to measure by re-taking assessments at prescribed intervals, thus giving the participant a clear picture of what needs to be done and when.

Integrated Assessment – Attitude, Skill, Knowledge

Figure 4.5   Effect of integrated or 360-degree assessment

FOR LINE MANAGEMENT

The benefits of KA for the line management are as follows.

- Perhaps the most important is that line management can plan entirely meaningful training and development programmes for their direct reports within a practical timescale to match business development objectives.

- HR will provide full support for these endeavours to the line management.

FOR HR

The benefits of KA for HR are as follows.

- The key point here is that HR will be in possession of assessment standards throughout the organization which are free of individual anomalies of approach and opinion.

- HR can also monitor repeat assessments and track training plans to ensure that they are carried out in a timely and efficient manner based upon complete commitment by individual participants and the line management.

FOR TOP MANAGEMENT

The benefits of KA for top management are as follows.

- Here's where the 'cream' of the benefits emerge as far as the direction that the company has chosen to take is concerned. A clear focus on managing the talent of the company becomes abundantly clear.

- Training budgets can be reduced by as much as 50 per cent because people are only trained in what they need to know for their current and identified future assignments. In a large enterprise with thousands of professional employees, this can mean significant cost savings every year.

SUMMARY

As has been said, knowledge assessment is a relatively new process but is gaining considerable momentum, as the so-called 'missing link' of integrated or 360-degree assessment.

Many organizations, small, medium or large, will not hire or undertake any form of training without an assessment of the knowledge base and development needs of individual business practitioners. With the advent of sophisticated technology, allowing hundreds, if not thousands, of participants to sit the assessments at any one time, with automatic and immediate distribution of evaluations and other reports, there is little question that KA will become the standard means by which knowledge and limitations in knowledge are clearly understood by everyone concerned in individual and group development.

Prescribed training through knowledge assessment is certainly a positive way forward for determining structured improvement programmes.

CASE STUDIES

CASE STUDY 1: HOW TO CHOOSE THE BEST CANDIDATE FROM THE SHORTLIST?

Situation

A major Government department had a vacancy for one senior project or programme manager to fill a new role in determining process strategy for a new application within a critical project. The department had carried out a number of interviews at both technical and business level and found that out of all of the potential candidates, four appeared to be eminently suitable for the assignment. First and second interviews had filtered out those who lacked the experience and capability to assume the new tasks, and a series of presentations and case exercises for the selected candidates had determined the correct balance of hard and soft skills required for the assignment. Psychometric testing had also been carried out to determine the behavioural characteristics of each candidate. The problem was: who was the best person for the job?

Key issues

One of the major points was that the candidate would need to be familiar with a number of tools and techniques within the project management body of knowledge.

These were:

- value management – the identification of the optimum solution using the lowest level of resource and cost without affecting the integrity of the solution;

- risk management – the analysis, evaluation and management of project risks;

- change control – the process of registering all potential changes in scope, specification, cost or schedule for review and approval before they are actioned.

Problems to overcome

There was just one problem – how do you really find out the knowledge level of potential candidates in these subjects within the total span of project management capability? Variable-content interviews are not enough; a standardized approach was indicated.

The solution

A means of assessing project management knowledge was needed and a suitable assessment instrument was used. The department decided to use a project management capability assessment and all four shortlisted candidates were instructed to go through the process. The assessment was completed within one hour under carefully controlled conditions so that there were no time overruns and everybody had an equal chance.

Outcome and benefits achieved

The results were very revealing. Of the four candidates, all of whom had been identified as being perfectly capable of doing the job, one was well below expectation in terms of detailed knowledge of the requirements; two were, at best, mediocre but one far exceeded expectations and was clearly the ideal candidate for the assignment. The major benefit of this exercise was that the risk of putting the wrong person into the job was minimized with a commensurate saving of further recruitment cost. Also, had the assessment been taken earlier, the amount of management time that have could have been saved would have been considerable.

Reinforcement programme to prevent future recurrence

First of all, it was decided that all shortlisted candidates should be assessed in this way far earlier in the recruitment process. Secondly, a training needs analysis was obtained as a by-product of the assessment to ensure that any knowledge gaps are plugged before they become major issues and thirdly, knowledge assessment is now added to the standard processes of measurement in addition to other forms of testing, for example psychometric.

CASE STUDY 2: HOW DO WE MAKE ROOM FOR MORE TALENT WHEN WE'RE FULLY UP TO HEADCOUNT?

Situation

A major clearing bank has a problem. They have over 4000 project and business analysis personnel but they know that at least 10 per cent of the people are performing at less than the standards required. At the other end of the scale, they are confident that a similar number of people are performing at an exceptional level. What they require is a definitive method of identifying those employees who could be released from the business, but HR are very concerned about any repercussions for any type of victimization or claims for wrongful dismissal. The bank clearly wants to attract, develop and retain top people but if there is no headcount relief, there appears to be little alternative but to carry out what is essentially a downsizing operation in order to replace unsatisfactory performers with more talented people. But the operation needs to be carried out with extreme sensitivity and care, coupled with unquestioned respect for the dignity of the individual employees concerned.

Key issues

Although it might not have been readily admitted, some people likely to be released might not have been clearly informed that their performance standards were not quite up to standard. For example, due to budget cuts, the amount and level of training provided to people who needed it had not been available and clearly many aspects of personal development had deteriorated. This would have affected the inexperienced and the marginal performers more than the higher-level performers.

Furthermore, performance appraisals had been very much along the lines of one-to-one interviews with the supervisor and employee, perhaps subject to a nominal monitoring by HR and senior line management at best.

Problems to overcome

Somehow, a programme had to be put into place without raising undue concerns or panic. 'Why am I on the programme? Why aren't you? What's it all about? Are they trying to get rid of me? Why wasn't I warned ages ago there was a problem?'

How could this programme be put in place to avoid something approaching anarchy? First of all, HR announced that there might be a call for voluntary redundancy. Secondly, due to headcount cuts some people would need to consider redeployment. A number of 'sweeteners' was also provided to help people come to terms with what was essentially the need to reduce headcount to make way for new talent.

The solution

Knowledge assessment on its own would not be enough. Neither would psychometric measurement. Both streams of input were required in order to produce a balanced assessment plus interviews in both disciplines. A psychometric testing consultancy and a company providing knowledge assessment and debrief interviews were invited to carry out the processes of assessment in parallel. The project was completed in seven weeks and, at the end, a comprehensive breakdown of results was formulated, with detailed analyses of 400 people who had been identified as 'downsizees'.

Outcome and benefits achieved

Of the 400 people on the programme, only 172 could be justified as being worthy of release. This was based upon the combined psychometric and knowledge assessments plus the personal interviews. This caused something of a problem for the identifiers of the 'notional' candidates. A further drill-down involving line management in addition to the original HR assessment became necessary to identify a further group of people. A further 300 people were invited to undergo the assessment process. By similar means of the first round, a total of 423 people, including the original 172, were named as being suitable for the downsizing exercise.

The benefits were very real. First of all, only those who could benefit from redeployment or release were positively identified, probably for their own benefit and secondly, most importantly, not one claim against the bank was made for any form of compensation, other than that originally offered by the bank as part of the release process. Finally, the bank had the headcount now to attract new talent and, as part of the selection and recruitment process, a dynamic means of assessment prior to making a commitment to hire.

Reinforcement programme to prevent future recurrence

One of the problems associated with the need to take this action may have been predicated upon a number of factors:

- inefficient recruitment standards in the first place
- insufficient training and development

- mediocre performance appraisal

- reluctance to confront unsatisfactory performance until necessary

- line managers taking the 'easy option' of avoiding exposure to the people they had hired.

So, how can this situation be avoided?

1. Use both psychometric and knowledge assessment before a hiring decision.

2. Use training needs analysis (TNA) to identify gaps in capability.

3. Verify the effectiveness of training after, say, six months, by further knowledge assessment.

4. Set up an effective performance appraisal system using people other than just the employee's supervisor (360-degree assessment).

5. Have the courage to identify the real capability of the people, whether they are recent hires or longer-term employees. It will save a lot of problems in the future.

CASE STUDY 3: IDENTIFYING REAL TALENT IN YOUR OWN ORGANIZATION

Situation

The CEO of a large company in the financial services industry asked her HR Director to carry out a skills inventory covering all managers, the sales force, project professionals and all other staff involved in customer service and support.

The CEO was aware of a significant gap between the known top performers and the rest of the work force but strongly suspected that the company had overlooked or inadvertently 'hidden' latent talent in many areas. Were the right people in the right jobs? An example might have been in the sales teams where perhaps New Business salespeople could have made better Account Managers and vice versa. Similarly, in the field of project management perhaps too much emphasis had been placed upon hard skills, that is formal methods and procedures, but employees' talent in soft skills, namely organization, people management and general management issues, had not been clearly identified. The way forward appeared to be that an inventory was necessary to isolate any evidence that could realign the correct assignments for all concerned.

Key issues

- First of all, this exercise would be a large undertaking and a firm implementation plan would need to be formulated and communicated to all employees under the signature of the CEO with a clear explanation as to why it was being carried out.

- In order to allay any fears and prevent 'gossip in the corridors', regular updates would need to be issued by way of 'CEO messages'.

- Process and milestone dates must be spelled out and strictly adhered to.

- An open-door policy encouraging employees to consult their management would need to be re-confirmed.

Problems to overcome

If there is a significant amount of untapped talent in the company, 1) how did this condition occur and 2) how will this be corrected without affecting the credibility of the management of the company in the eyes of its employees?

The solution

The HR Director, named as 'Project Manager' for this exercise, formulated a plan to address all the issues and dependencies with the following key events:

- Firstly, to carry out a survey of known top performers to find out their attitudes, opinions and successful working methods. This was to be handled by way of a specially designed questionnaire, followed up by a personal interview by both internal managers and external consultants.

- The next step would be to collate the results by function to determine common themes that could form the basis of a model that could be used to establish the most successful profiles.

- Then a knowledge assessment programme would be implemented to assess the capability of salespeople, project professionals, business analysts, relationship managers, graduate intakes and first- and second-line managers.

- Care would be taken to ensure that current assignments were very clearly defined, so that any deviations could readily be analysed and recommendations for realignment could be made to the CEO and the board.

Outcome and benefits achieved

The CEO's original view was largely upheld. The results of the initial survey conducted with known top performers revealed a regular pattern of operational methods and personal preferences that proved to distinguish outstanding from just good performance.

The output from the knowledge assessments, read in conjunction with HR records and appraisal interviews conducted by line managers, showed the following:

1. 23 per cent of the sales force were assigned to tasks for which they were not best suited, probably as a result of poorly set targets requiring 'warm bodies' in the wrong jobs rather than matching talent to real needs.

2. 9 per cent of project professionals were incorrectly graded. Those with the strongest soft skills had not been recognized for their management capability – only technical prowess, some of whom did not even meet technical requirements.

3. 72 per cent of Business Analysts had never been assessed in their own field; instead they were measured as project personnel, a role for which they could not have possibly met all-round requirements.

4. Graduate intakes had been given the role of 'management trainee'. 67 per cent of them lacked any knowledge of teamwork, conflict management or presentation skills.

5. 84 per cent of Relationship Managers lacked integral skills, for example business orientation was unmatched by product and service knowledge and vice versa.

As a result of this revelation, the CEO decided to implement a re-orientation training programme for all those affected by the findings.

Specially designed training modules were established with a planned programme of management monitoring and re-assessment after six months.

When the programme reached its logical conclusion, productivity within the company rose by 26 per cent in terms of increased revenue and commensurate profitability – all because the company identified untapped talent and reassigned it to the best and most productive areas of the business, matched by the best people with the optimum talent for the job.

Reinforcement programme to prevent future recurrence

In future, all new hires and candidates for promotion would be carefully matched against precise job descriptions, using knowledge assessment techniques incorporating competency selection to ensure that only relevant categories were assessed for the current and any known future assignment.

A training management system would be produced to provide automatic notices of attendance for all personnel on the programme, and HR would be given the responsibility to monitor smooth running and compliance with the process.

The company emerged from this exercise with a great deal of kudos. All the employees, apart from a small minority, felt that the organization was committed to pursuing the highest possible standards and results but, at the same time, making sure that the individual employee was given every opportunity to develop and advance.

CHAPTER 5

Education and Training

EDUCATION

Companies running talent development programmes soon realize that they need to develop top-quality people who can lead and motivate others to achieve the highest levels of productivity and, hence, performance.

There are a number of factors that are important in achieving top-level results, but perhaps the main ones are to develop and sustain outstanding ability in business strategy, stewardship and management of change.

It has been said that talented people have an innate capability for recognizing opportunity, seizing it and making it happen. So the critical contributors to such achievement are:

- managing teams of people

- identifying value and ensuring its delivery

- sound short-, medium- and long-term decision-making

- appraising performance and taking corrective action in a consistent manner

- managing and reinforcing change programmes.

Essentially, this means identifying the education culture of the organization and its people, and for top performers this will mean concentrating upon the following issues in order to develop a well-rounded business professional:

- market and product/services strategy

- manufacturing or process know-how

- distribution channels

- supply-chain management

- operational issues

- financial considerations including pricing strategy.

Of course, there are other factors involved, but it is important to realize that, traditionally, managers and other professionals, even on a fast-track promotion programme, tended to know their specific discipline, for example marketing, sales or technical support, but lacked the 'completeness' of linked functions representing the total span of the business.

Within the current concept of talent management, education issues now cover many more skills, enabling participants to *ask and answer* such issues as:

- How do costs and expenses flow through our company?

- What does our cash flow position indicate?

- As we're in a state of rapid growth, does this guarantee us increased value?

Clearly, this implies that people identified as participants on the programme have attended more than just a 'Finance for non-Finance managers' course.

This means that the type of education needed will cover such subjects as:

- value theory and earned value analysis

- cost of capital

- discounted cash flow

- project evaluation

- risk management.

One of the main reasons for this more comprehensive education approach is that the type of people we are describing will need to act upon specialist recommendations from highly-skilled staff groups, for example Finance, Legal, Business practices, Contracts – in the full knowledge that the decisions made will need to be solid, based upon considered assessments and the capability to understand the technical issues involved.

Finally, on this question of education culture, meaningful programmes will include, amongst other factors:

- development of knowledge of self-awareness

- understanding the true motivation of interpersonal communication contacts

- strategy for effective problem-solving.

Clearly some of the tools already identified in Chapter 3 will be of great use in applying the desired education programmes. For example, to enable those on the talent management fast-track programme to better manage their people, an understanding of their preferred Belbin team roles, their differing personality types (Myers-Briggs, Saville and Holdsworth and so on) and their preferred learning styles will all be advantageous. As a precursor to this, improved self-awareness of their own profiles is, of course, a necessity.

TRAINING

Within any company there is always the question of which is best: running training programmes with an internal training department, using line managers to train their own staff or using external specialist companies? The answer which the majority of companies come to is to use a combination of all three.

However, the experience of the authors, who have worked with many hundreds of companies, is that there is an inherent danger in exposing employees on fast-track talent management programmes to standard courses developed many years previously by people other than those now delivering them.

Internal training is not normally a position occupied by the most ambitious or enthusiastic employees. As you will see below, it is difficult to run professional and motivational training courses. It is not desirable, therefore, to send your most talented people to an event that will at best disappoint them and at worse make them resentful of time wasted.

The answer is that if for economic reasons an internal training department is deemed necessary, then the courses should be regularly updated and reviewed by senior management. Secondly, working in the training department should be a temporary career move made by employees on the talent management programme who want to be seen to be helping their career by honing their technical and presentation skills.

With regards to using line managers to train staff, this can be effective if they are given proper guidance. Therefore, in this section of the Chapter, we have attempted to provide three very important elements of training specifically for those assigned to a talent management programme.

1.   Management Guide to running successful training courses internally.

2.   Outline of a relevant training workshop dealing with improving interpersonal relationships including dealing with difficult people.

3.   Perhaps the most important skill of all – presenting and achieving change.

MANAGEMENT GUIDE TO RUNNING SUCCESSFUL TRAINING COURSES INTERNALLY

INTRODUCTION

This management guide has been compiled to enable managers to plan and deliver modular training for their professional staff on a talent management programme.

Any programme that consists of presentations and detailed transcripts can be used in any combination to provide effective training with the minimum amount of preparation.

This guide will help managers to supervise various types of training events from self-study to formal group sessions.

The guide covers the following agenda:

- aims and objectives
- organization
- execution
- technique
- attitude
- decorum
- follow-up.

It should be read through thoroughly before beginning to plan any event.

The basis of the training requirements will be some form of appropriate knowledge assessment in order to determine the up-to-date training needs analysis. This will not always be necessary as the line or training manager responsible will no doubt have identified certain training requirements based upon observation, for example, during normal business activity.

AIM AND OBJECTIVES

Every training event should have a strategic aim and specific objectives which will be achieved as a result of participation.

1. *Definition of aim*: this will normally be a global statement that is based upon the provision of a forum for learning a new set of skills. For example, on a sales training workshop for selected participants, if a sales trainee is required to learn the basics of qualification skills, then the aim would be 'to provide a forum for learning how to maximize productivity in sales and to eliminate, as far as possible, those prospects who have no intention of buying from us'. The aim, therefore, is not the process but the strategic result that we are seeking.

2. *Objectives*: these are very specific and follow the subject matter very closely by adding knowledge to the key areas to be covered. To take the same example as above, the objectives might be: as a result of completing this training module you will be able to:

   a) determine whether or not the proposed sales project is viable;

   b) determine whether we have a possibility of gaining the business;

   c) apply a variety of qualification parameters at the right time, with the right emphasis;

   d) appreciate the continuing process of qualification throughout the sales cycle;

   e) recognize when to re-qualify at different levels;

   f) understand the correlation between qualification, objection handling and closing as an integrated process.

ORGANIZATION

No training course organizes itself, but by using a simple but effective structure the event can be run efficiently with the minimum amount of preparation. The key points within the structure are as follows:

1. *Administration*: confirm either verbally or by email when the training is to be carried out and what precisely is to be covered (produce an agenda if appropriate).

2. *Environment*: where is the training to take place? This will depend upon the type of event, for example self-study can be left to the individual to arrange in his or her spare time at home, or a more formal process will require the booking of a training room or even off-site premises, should that be indicated.

3. *Facilities*: what equipment will be required? Most training rooms have provision for running presentations via a permanent projector installation, or perhaps an individual can just use a desktop or a notebook to run the necessary presentations. If it is a larger group and such things as whiteboards and marker pens are necessary, make sure that they are available.

4. *Structure*: this will be determined by the extent of the training programme. An informal 'I think you had better brush up on objection handling' does not require much in the way of structure but a group session probably will, in which case timetables and key events need to be specified in the agenda (see (1) above).

5. *Material*: as far as this programme is concerned, the manager will need to provide the participant(s) with the necessary training materials to complete the task and in order to ensure that the material movement is properly monitored, a log book should be kept showing date of release and date returned.

6. *Course evaluation form*: a simple form can be devised for completion for the participant(s) so that regular feedback is obtained regarding use and effectiveness of the programme. A sample form is given in Appendix A.

EXECUTION

This will vary widely depending upon the type of event. If we take, as an example, a one-day event for five salespeople covering, perhaps, three competencies, the following suggestions are worthy of note:

1. *Timetable*: have a clear indication of start and finish times and particularly provide advance notice of any evening work that may be necessary, for example associated case studies or product updates.

2. *Breaks*: on a standard training course you may consider the following to be acceptable: coffee on arrival, 9:00 start, 10:30–10:45 coffee break, 12:30–1:15 lunch break (specify precise arrangements for lunch, for example outside caterer bringing in working buffet lunch), 3:00–3:15 tea break, 5:30 end of formal session with half

hour break before syndicate work from, say, 6:00–7:30. End of workshop.

3.   *Facilities for practical exercises*: if there is some syndicate work to do, ensure that syndicate rooms are available to cover the appropriate timescales.

4.   *Reporting procedures*: explain precisely how the information to be gained is reported back, for example informal presentation? Open discussion/brainstorming? Whatever the case, make sure people know what is expected of them.

THE TRAINER'S ATTITUDE

If you are to conduct the training session yourself and you have a limited experience in conducting training events, the following notes might help:

1.   Even though you may be the participants' manager, training is different from day-to-day managing. Clearly you have to be authoritative but open-minded where new material is being covered and different people may have different rates of absorption.

2.   Don't forget to sell, rather than tell, difficult issues. As the instructor, you are the bringer of new knowledge and skills, and if you conduct the workshop in a professional manner you will be seen as the source of the information, rather than just the purveyor.

3.   Exercise a great deal of patience with questions from your audience. There is no such thing as a silly question but there are plenty of silly answers and under no circumstances should you attempt to minimize the importance of an issue raised by a less experienced course participant.

However, you must at all times be sensitive to the other participants and not concentrate too much on one person. You should also ensure that any personal issues which might only affect an individual questioner are taken offline, wherever possible.

Remember also that in any group of course participants some will be stronger than others, and your job is to remain sensitive to the needs of the weaker participants without boring those who are racing through the material!

Identify any difficult candidate(s) and get them on your side as quickly as possible. Otherwise you might find that a negative attitude purports, which can quickly spread to the rest of the group. (One particularly effective approach is to solicit their opinion on some difficult subjects prior to a wider group discussion. Where possible you can then build on their 'good' ideas.)

An inexperienced trainer sometimes finds it amusing to pick on one particular participant. You will not receive any medals from anyone for doing so!

Above all, look as though you are enjoying yourself and that will also rub off on the course participants.

TECHNIQUE

The technique involved is somewhat different for an internal sales manager as opposed to that of an external trainer, but there are still some areas that need to be clearly established. In the event that you might be conducting a workshop that might involve other managers' people then your role will be more similar to that of an external trainer and therefore the following notes may help:

1.   For those who do not already know you, give them a *brief* thumbnail sketch of your background and position in the company.

2.   For those whom you do not know, elicit from them their own background.

3.   Outline the agenda in the following structure 2, 3, 4, 5 and 1. The reason for this is that it prevents us from saying the first part of the programme twice. An example might be 'in front of you, you will find a copy of today's agenda and, as you will see, we will be looking at the importance of qualification followed by objection handling, closing business and principles of account management – but we shall be starting with an outline of general sales and buying cycles'.

4.   In putting together the training programme you should ensure that there is cohesive progression from one subject to the next by using the technique known as 'linking'. In other words, explain the reasons for the move to the next subject on the agenda linking it closely to the reasons why the sequence of events has been designed in this way.

5.   A good trainer will regularly check for understanding. There is probably nothing worse than a sea of blank faces when you are trying to put over new points. Lack of participation generally implies lack of interest or your message has been blocked in some way. It

is your responsibility to ensure that the people get the most out of the training and therefore, in some cases, you will need to do some 'priming'. After you have made a point that is clearly a new facet of the subject matter under discussion, ask if there are any questions. If there are none and this is quite a common occurrence, say, 'what I am normally asked at this stage is...' This would generally start things moving and once the initial questions have been raised, they become self-generating.

6.   If someone makes a good point regarding, perhaps, a different angle but expressing a clear understanding of what you are presenting, pay the person concerned a compliment and make sure the rest of the class know why such a compliment was made. It can be very gratifying when conducting a training course to see that people are responding positively and that fact should be properly encouraged without overdoing it.

7.   As in any other management task, adhering strictly to time is one of the key paths to success of a training event. People are impressed by good time keeping. This does not mean you should rush through everything in order to finish at exactly the time you had announced, but do not let things drag on unnecessarily. If, for example, it is nearly lunchtime and you have not even finished the first module your audience will become more and more involved in trying to work out the ultimate finish time and the training effectiveness will have become diluted.

8.   One of the best ways of ensuring adherence to time promises is to remind people of the agenda at various intervals. This technique is called signposting. You owe it to your audience to let them know where they are, in order to get the best in terms of the investment of their time.

9.   Finally, do not allow any interruptions unless they are of an urgent personal nature. Arrange messages to be placed on a message board outside the training room to be picked up at the next break and, most importantly, ensure that people return promptly after the breaks for the next session.

DECORUM

The golden rule of formality that normally applies in any form of external presentation can be bought into the internal classroom. You are the person in charge and therefore you should adopt a fairly formal approach because of the serious nature of the training; however, you should allow more informality as the audience becomes relaxed during the course of the event. This does not mean, however, that you relinquish in any way your authority but there is no need to stand on ceremony either. Perhaps the best way of describing it would be to adopt the 'velvet glove' approach i.e. a positive attitude but very much to the point.

A few points of clarification:

1.   Maintain the appropriate distance but in a friendly manner.

2.   Dress in accordance with the company's guidelines but, essentially, be smart in appearance and 'look the part'.

3.   Under no circumstances make any remarks whatsoever which could be described as being politically incorrect or derogatory against any person.

4.   By all means introduce humour but do not let it get out of hand and do not spend ten minutes on the latest jokes you might have heard the night before. Humour must be in good taste and remember, as a manager/trainer you have what is called 'referent power'. This means that less experienced and worldly people will follow your example, both good and bad types. At the end of the workshop, if appropriate, distribute the course evaluation forms if you are using them and ensure the participants complete them there and then and hand them back. You will want to know what they thought about the course content and the way it was delivered (see Appendix A).

5.   If appropriate, provide participants with a contact point for queries (if some of the people do not report directly to you).

6.   In some companies, HR requires formal notice of attendance and completion. If so, distribute these as well.

7.   Prepare a debrief document for your own management for you to report back on the way in which the training was carried out and provide a brief cameo of each person's performance with recommendations for future involvement. At the same time, highlight any immediate issues or concerns that need attention.

8.   Carry out a post-course interview with the participants and check for the effectiveness of the training by carefully selecting appropriate questions.

9.   If a pre-course knowledge assessment tool was used, it will be useful to ask the trainees to take the same assessment, say, three months after the course to measure the improvement in retained knowledge about the subject.

TITLE OF MODULE: NEGOTIATING WITH DIFFICULT PEOPLE

The following module provides an illustration of an internal training module conducted by an internal line manager, designed for project professionals on a fast-track talent management programme.

Aim: To provide a forum for various levels of project professional staff and managers to experience the ways in which different people, with different objectives and different agendas, can be handled in order to progress the project in a controlled manner.

Objectives: As a result of attendance, participants will be able to:

- use new negotiating skills involving various types of personal qualities required to be successful

- reach win/win status

- establish clear working relationships

- reduce any vestiges of resentment on either side

- go forward in a very positive manner to achieve tactical and strategic objectives for the project.

All this will be structured in a framework covering the various types of personality and attitude displayed by people who are creating various types of blockages. This will enable the participant to handle people who may have some or all of the following characteristics:

- pre-conceived ideas

- lack of motivation

- refusal to accept contrary data

- misinterpretation of information (deliberate or otherwise)

- doubts about the credibility of the source of information

- perceived lack of communication skills

- hiding behind complexity of channels.

Pre-requisites: None

Duration: Two days

Attendees:

1. Alex Davis – London HQ

2. Maddy Joseph – Paris Nord

3. Katie Angelina – Rome Marketing Competence Centre

4. Summer Cate – Geneva Distribution Centre

5. Oscar Fairfax-Scott – Manufacturing, White Plains, NY.

Method: The module will be based upon a mixture of theory and practical sessions that will comprise an agenda as follows:

1. Introduction, aims and objectives

2. Basic communication skills

3. The need for sound interpersonal skills

4. The problem of media distortion.

All of the above will be illustrated by easy-to-follow graphics of the various processes and models that take place during communication.

1. Introduction to negotiation skills

   This will be based upon extracts from a well-established existing training module, comprehensively customized to our specific business requirements, which will cover items such as buyer's tactics, negotiating frameworks, types of negotiation, suggested strategies and outline of personal skills.

2. Profiles of the various contacts in project management in day-to-day dealings

   In this session we shall cover the important characteristics of the following types of people:

   - internal senior management

   - client senior management

   - external consultants

- internal staff groups (for example, finance, legal, marketing)

- peer groups

- resource managers

- subordinates

- third party contractors.

These profiles will be based upon expected reactions of people in the above positions and the way they generally operate.

SKILL REHEARSALS

The practical part of this workshop will be provided in the form of role-play briefs in which the instructor will play the part of a designated contact for which a written brief is prepared and the participant will play the part of, say, the project manager, who will be attempting to achieve the objectives laid down in his or her written briefing document.

Typical examples of these might be as follows:

NEGOTIATING WITH YOUR MANAGER

Participant brief

Your project is beginning to slip slightly and you have assessed the fact that the resources currently at your disposal, if not increased temporarily, could result in irrecoverable delay to the delivery of the end product. You have on occasion mentioned this to your manager, who is responsible for the whole programme, but have received little practical advice or response from him. He has hinted on occasion that you tend to worry too much in advance and has even suggested that you occasionally 'cry wolf'. This has resulted in a somewhat neutral relationship between you and the programme manager. Nevertheless, you do not have the authority to authorize further resources for your project so you are very much in the hands of your boss. You have set up a meeting with him specifically to ask for two C++ programmers for two months in order to regain the slippage that is beginning to be caused. Your manager is a stickler for detail and you know that he requires chapter and verse in order to approve such requests. You should prepare thoroughly for this meeting, as your credibility might be further on the line.

Instructor brief

The instructor will have a complementary brief which may also contain one or two 'surprises' which the participant will need to handle in improvisation mode.

INTERNAL MANAGEMENT BRIEFING WITH THE IT DIRECTOR

Participant brief

You are a project manager responsible for a strategic project that is of dynamic interest to your divisional director. He has requested a short briefing on the current status of the project. You have welcomed the opportunity that this session will provide because you have discovered during your implementation of the project some techniques and procedural changes that could be of value to future such projects and your immediate manager fully approves of the innovations that you have uncovered. The purpose in meeting your director will be twofold: (a) to provide a progress report; and (b) to present your innovations. You have only met the director a couple of times before, passing in the corridor for maybe just a brief chat, but this will be the first opportunity that you will have had to meet him in such a structured environment. You should remember that his assessment of you up to now will have been based upon reports that he has received from your management, plus superficial observation, therefore the planned session will be very important to you. The only personal characteristics that you know of the director is that he has a reputation for having preconceived ideas and difficulty in accepting concepts that he has not initiated himself. This does *not* mean that he has a complete closed mind but your manager advises you that he will be looking for not only strength in substance but also in style and structure. You will have time to prepare a meaningful outline sketch of your project.

Instructor brief

An instructor will play the part of the director but also your manager, another participant in the group, will also be present. The instructor will have a fairly straightforward brief and is looking for establishment and maintenance of the credibility of the project manager he is about to meet. Being a very senior manager, he will no doubt throw in a few 'curvers' and his interest level will be binary, that is, very interested or completely turned off and he will no doubt display these characteristics during the meeting. There are no catches or pitfalls but this particular briefing session is highly typical of the ways in which top management operate.

GENERAL

Depending upon the actual number of participants, everyone will have an opportunity to practise the skills necessary and as everyone will be observing everyone else, the total learning experience will be common to all. Preparation for each of the 'meetings' will be done in syndicate groups but everyone will have a chance to participate in the role-plays.

Each participant will have a complete set of course notes covering both the theory and practice for future reference. Furthermore, a brief note will be issued in advance of the course to focus attention upon the type of workshop e.g. residential involving evening work. An example is below:

> *The workshop will be held at the Hilton Hotel, New Town, UK. Full joining instructions and notification of expense allocation will be issued within the next 14 days. The workshop will be residential for all participants. Adequate time will be provided for syndicate work but substantial evening work will be involved.*

PRESENTING CHANGE

One of the most important attributes of someone on a talent management programme is the ability to present change in a structured manner.

INTRODUCTION

Presenting a proposal for change is completely different from presenting, say, a technical dissertation. The key factor to remember is that you are asking people to change their current working methods and to adopt your ideas. By its very nature, a change presentation will be highly interactive (if it is to be of any value) and will be full of different views, objections and reservations that emanate from the audience. The value in presenting the proposal for change is that it gives the presenter the opportunity to gauge the reaction to the written proposal or internal report, without allowing the written document alone to do the selling.

By its very nature, a proposal for change requires considerable planning and preparation time. As a guideline, a presentation lasting one hour, including questions, could take anything from six to eight hours to prepare.

This outline will cover both external presentations, for example to customers and prospects or user departments (Part 1) and internal management briefings (Part 2), plus a separate session on some elements of presentation technique.

PRIMARY CONSIDERATIONS

The presenter is the change agent or catalyst, whose job it is to speed up the process of acceptance of change. Just because an employee may know the subject inside out, this does not mean that people can be induced to change their current working methods readily. The presenter's attitudes must be realistic, based upon reasoned argument, containing practical recommendations and, most importantly, with plenty of confidence and enthusiasm.

STRATEGY FOR CHANGE – KEY ISSUES

There are always five issues irrespective of the subject matter of the change being presented and they are as follows:

1.   What is the proposal?

2.   What is wrong with the present situation?

3.   How will the proposed solution work?

4.   How much will it all cost?

5.   What are the benefits?

Each of these issues requires a systematic approach. Let's refer to them as the five steps for presenting a proposal for change.

PART 1: PREPARING A PROPOSAL FOR CHANGE TO CUSTOMERS AND PROSPECTS

- *Step 1: What is the proposal?*

   In this section, you state your objectives and your understanding of the prospect's requirements and objectives. This is something of a scene-setter which enables you to get off to a good start (providing you have got it right!). This section is normally covered by an agenda which is displayed in visual form throughout the presentation, either by handout or in screen form.

- *Step 2: What is wrong with the present situation?*

   Extreme care must be taken in this step not to talk about the problems of the prospect because criticism, at this stage, will not be easily digested. The way to handle this is to talk about the current situation in terms of needs. For example, it would be wrong to say, if we were selling a stock control system, that stock levels are inordinately high. It would be much better to talk about the need to optimize stock levels to match customer service requirements. A further word of caution – all facts must be checked thoroughly for accuracy and relevance. Your audience will be only too keen to pounce upon any mis-statements or generalizations and the whole presentation can be destroyed by some inadvertent and careless comment regarding, say, volumes.

- *Step 3: How will the proposed solution work?*

Here we are effectively presenting the beginning of a solution, but we are in essence stating what must be done to remedy the situation. It is in this step where the sensitivity of the presenter comes to the fore. A very professional and highly advisable approach might be to present alternatives, giving reasons for selection of the optimum solution and rejection of those that do not quite provide the best answers. This may be done in the following form: 'After carefully looking into your requirements, we found that there are three possible approaches, solutions a, b and c'. You then go on to define the solutions and then eliminate the two less desirable options and finish with your specific recommendation. It goes without saying that your solution must relate completely to the user's needs, and we are talking about real needs, as opposed to perceived needs. Many presentations fail because we present what we thought the prospect wanted, but other parts of the business have other requirements and we may not know the real priorities. That is why we emphasize real needs; those that are acknowledged to be the strategic requirements. One more point – and very important ones: any implementation issues must be handled effectively and realistically. An example of this might be a large file conversion job. If a member of the audience says 'We have 420 000 spare-parts records to put onto our new stock control system' – don't say, 'I had no idea there were so many' or even worse 'That is not a problem!'

Remember the mention of implementation issues at this stage should be regarded as a possible positive reaction and should be encouraged and probably handled by reference to a similar exercise carried out successfully elsewhere. Another factor involved in this is very interesting from a psychological standpoint. Once you have obtained tacit agreement that your solution is likely to be acceptable, at least in principle, address the decision-maker if they are present with some words along the following lines: 'I would like to take this opportunity of saying how much assistance we obtained during our survey of the requirements from Jim and Sally – not only did they provide us with all the information we required, but with their knowledge of the requirements and the capability of the solution we have jointly produced, you will end up with a very advanced process which will give you that extra competitive edge which you have been seeking including a clear path for achieving your primary objective of increasing market share.' Just think about these words for one moment – we are not talking about a solution; we are talking about our solution which is a joint, unique production. The decision-makers want to feel that they are in safe hands. If there is a solution constituted by a team who can provide the right solution, the proposer is likely to be well on the way to a successful conclusion.

- *Step 4: How much will it cost?*

An important point to cover in this step is that costs must include everything. For example, you may be providing hardware and software for an IT solution, but you should also ensure that maintenance costs are carefully spelt out and any 'linked costs' such as telecommunications should be at least mentioned in outline, because the prospect will be paying for everything, not necessarily only your section of the system proposal. You do not have to be an expert in other suppliers' costings, but at least show that you are aware of and sensitive to the total budget involvement particularly if you are in a position to sell financial benefits.

Talking about benefits, try to reach the point where you can address agreed potential quantifiable benefits. This means that you will probably have been through a process of agreeing with the user's finance people that savings on inventory can realistically be expected to be at least, say, 15 per cent of current value, that the savings are clearly only potential in that they have not yet been achieved, but have been clearly illustrated by reference to a similar user, that the savings are clearly quantifiable in that a figure can be established showing tangible levels of saving and finally that it will be a benefit, which normally means savings in time and/or money.

If you are able, and you really know what you are talking about, you can even talk to finance people about return on investment and internal rate of return and other similar project appraisal terms.

- *Step 5: What are the benefits?*

  As intimated in the previous step, tangible benefits are measurable in advance and intangible benefits can be set up for ongoing monitoring. Examples of tangible benefits are, as illustrated before, reductions in inventory and also job throughput performance improvement, staff redeployment and so on. Intangible benefits are quite different; here we would be talking about increase in market share, improved customer service levels, better response times, competitive edge, as just a few examples. Intangible benefits are those that can be measured after a planned period to see what the effect of the change has been. It does not require much imagination to see how useful it would be if the CEO of an organization who has used your recommendations could say after one year that he has improved market share by 12.5 per cent. The follow-up and analysis of the results showing a substantial benefit of such results will be a major responsibility of a participant on a talent management programme, simply because such candidates are being groomed to be the beneficiaries of such achievement.

PART 2: PREPARING AND PRESENTING CHANGE TO INTERNAL SENIOR MANAGEMENT

The important point to remember here is that the strategy for change is identical but the 'cosmetics', that is, style and structure may well change. Let's have a look at some of the key issues.

- *Objectives*

  A properly structured internal management briefing should enable us to obtain decisions faster, always providing, of course, that we address the correct group of recommenders, influencers and decision-makers.

  A well-structured briefing has been proven over and over again to be a much more effective use of everyone's time – that is, if everyone likely to be affected by the change(s) is present, this leads to better communication faster.

  Not only that, whether we like it or not, we are judged, in terms of our professional credibility and hence development, by our ability to sell internally. We will inevitably be measured, in terms of future opportunity, on the basis of the quality of presentations we make internally. To put it another way, senior management are looking for future senior managers and if we deliver consistent understanding and credibility, we become the focus of attention for future moves within the company.

- *General observation*

It is very important that we understand that we are not there just to impart information and answer questions. On the contrary, we should have completed our 'staff work' in order to show our understanding of new business requirements or opportunity. Therefore, it is very important that substance, style and structure are held at the highest possible levels. Unfortunately, it is often the case that substance, that is the content of the presentation, is sound but style and structure do not quite match the importance of the message and these factors can materially affect our personal credibility.

- *Internal presentation principles*

Curiously enough, we start with the answer. An example might be:

'John [senior executive], ladies and gentlemen, I seek your approval today to open a new branch in Manchester because of the increasing business volumes which cannot be handled satisfactorily on a remote basis.'

In this case, the presenter is seeking approval for a new facility and makes it quite clear what the goal is. As can be imagined, a great deal of data will need to be provided together with a risk assessment and therefore the mainline visuals will need to be backed up by detailed visuals, if necessary to the tune of about 40 per cent. That is, 40 per cent of mainline visuals will probably require detailed back-up.

In an audience of the type described above, the presenter may find it difficult to exercise the control that he or she would like to. It must be emphasized that it is very important to do so otherwise the audience can take over control – particularly some of the minor members of the audience who may be there to prove a point.

One other issue: allow plenty of interaction, at the same time ensuring that the most senior person present is not 'losing it' or becoming bored by show-offs airing their knowledge. Every so often, make sure that you bring the audience back to the main line of the message. Let's have a look at all of these in a bit more detail:

- *Start with the answer*

The key point here is that this forces a precise statement of the business issue and makes it absolutely clear what is being proposed. It may be pertinent in certain circumstances to provide a very brief history of issues that have caused the need for change and this can be conveniently coupled with 'why you are here'.

Also make it quite clear the type of response that you are looking for. Is it approval? A formal decision? Support for further investigation? Or just information and approval to proceed further should the interest level generated during the presentation become sufficiently high?

The example that has been given above, regarding the opening of a new office, is just one of many. You could be asking for an increase in headcount, new demonstration facilities, more admin support, replacement equipment, approval to bid for a major business situation requiring resources outside of your control. Whatever the situation – the process is very similar.

- *Back-up v. mainline visuals*

Senior management are notorious for identifying that aspect of your proposal for change that you failed to 'staff-out' as well as you might have done. This may have been due to time constraints or simply lack of information. Always try to avoid going to senior management with incomplete staff work because you will find it very difficult to obtain a satisfactory conclusion in the absence of all the information required to make a decision. This is not just a matter of a complete assessment of the business requirement – this is what also affects that magic word: your credibility. Most people only meet their senior management on a few occasions throughout the year on a formal basis and the opportunity to shine when given the chance must not be underestimated. Therefore, do as much work as you possibly can to ensure you have, if not all, as many of the answers as your senior management might need.

When it comes to the use of back-up visuals, do not use them as a matter of course but only if called upon to do so. You may display a set of figures on your screen which cover, say, costs and sales for the last six months. You can be absolutely certain that if there are any surprises in any of those figures the senior person will want to know why. For example, if costs suddenly rose in month three of six, as displayed on the screen, do not under any circumstances imagine that you can get away with 'I'm not quite sure why'. Have the back-up visual aids readily available, suitably filed and indexed so that you can immediately recall them in the most professional manner.

- *Control of presentation*

This mostly relates to the cosmetic and the way in which your work will be perceived as a professional offering. If you are using a data-projector and one of your initial slides has the agenda on it, make sure you have separate printouts for each member of the audience so that they can follow the agenda at appropriate times. This may not always be the case but, generally speaking, an important presentation will have a written agenda. Do not forget to tell the audience, by reference to the agenda, which aspects you will be covering or not covering as an integral part of your presentation.

Be very precise about what it is that you want. Do not go for ill-defined agreements or ones which are likely to be changed once you are out of the room. Make it absolutely clear the scale and scope of the 'order' that you have in mind.

If your audience is interested (and the example will be set by the most senior person present), questions will flow and you will be interrogated, sometimes quite rigorously, therefore you will need to be able to improvise correct answers based upon the work that you have done, the support you have received during the investigation phase and the experiences that you have had. Do not try to answer vague or ill-defined questions. Try to force precision into each question while still maintaining the best possible relationship with your audience.

- *Obtain some order*

Throughout the presentation, bear in mind (and this is something some people lose sight of occasionally) that the objective is to gain some form of approval – not to give a presentation. Most 'internal' presenters have suffered from this delusion from time to time.

If, for reasons beyond your control, you are only able to settle for a partial or conditional decision, do so with good grace. You can be almost certain that this situation has arisen due to incomplete staff work. Once you detect that that is as much as you are going to get, do not push too hard or you could be in danger of making a thorough nuisance of yourself. Summarize outstanding actions still to be taken by name or function, together with completion dates where applicable, and mention that you will be minuting these items and distributing them to all members of the audience for follow-up purposes.

Summarize your precise understanding of what you have achieved. Do not assume anything at all and obtain agreement there and then that your summary reflects a true understanding of the position reached. Depending upon individual circumstances, it may be necessary to confirm in writing the agreement reached.

• *Presentation technique*

And now we come to the final part, technique. In the main, the process is common to both external and internal presentations. We will be looking at five different areas in this section, the introduction and the conclusion of the presentation, audience contact, use of visuals and control of mannerisms. First of all a question – what is more difficult to achieve successfully, the introduction or the conclusion of a presentation? When this question is asked in a training course, there will be a 50/50 response. Half will say introduction, the other half – conclusion. The reason why most people feel the Introduction is more difficult is because they think that you have to set up your credibility right at the beginning. This is very true; but your introduction can be rehearsed. The conclusion can also be rehearsed assuming that you conclude in the right place! But more often than not, there will be outstanding issues that need to be resolved before an effective conclusion can be reached and therefore, by definition, conclusions often have to be improvised. On balance, it is generally now agreed that the conclusion is the more difficult section to handle effectively. We will now take each of these issues regarding technique in turn.

Introduction

Make a clear, well-rehearsed start, taking charge of proceedings and introduce yourself, your company and your objectives. In a customer presentation this could take the following form:

> 'Good morning ladies and gentlemen, my name is Alex Davis, and I am Senior Partner at Tele International. As you know, we are in the

business of prescribed training using knowledge testing techniques and my objective today is to seek your approval to proceed with the personal development programme that both our companies have been working on over the last three months.'

You can then go to talk about the 'agenda issues' such as:

'The presentation will last one hour, after which we shall have a break for coffee and this session will be followed by a demonstration of the new test simulation that we have jointly developed, for those who have not yet seen it. Please feel free to ask questions at any time during the presentation. I have, of course, allowed time for questions at the end of the formal session, but if there are any issues which are fundamental to your basic understanding of what I am saying, please feel free to chip in at any time.'

The point worth noting about this last statement is that in an hierarchical presentation that is multi-level, you do not want too many low-level interruptions covering detail. The presentation should ideally be pitched at the most senior person present or, paradoxically, the lowest level of knowledge! If you find that you are getting bogged down in detail, suggest that the questions are valid but 'let us give them the time they deserve at the end of the presentation'.

Audience contact

A few pointers on this section – do not concentrate on only one section of the audience too much – the rest of the people will become irritated. Make sure that you maintain eye-to-eye contact with everyone in turn and that they are aware that you are doing so. Watch out for inattention, for example bored expressions, doodling or looking out of the window. If any of these conditions occur, try immediately to regain attention by asking a question or changing the texture of the presentation. However, care must be taken not to embarrass anyone in the presence of his or her colleagues and probably seniors. For example, do not say, 'what is your view on this, John?' if it is manifestly clear that John has not been listening for the last ten minutes, because you will not make any friends by causing embarrassment. If you suspect that John needs to be brought back into the main thrust of the presentation, carefully say 'Do you remember last week when we discussed this, your view was...?' John might not even know that you have let him off the hook! Changing the texture of the presentation generally means switching something off. This could mean an image on the screen, the computer, the lights, the sound or something to re-alert people to the next session in the presentation.

Visuals

Presentation media have changed somewhat in the last few years. At one time it was all flip-charts, then it became overhead transparencies followed by 35 mm slides, videos and even movies, all designed to help support the verbal message. Most people today use some form of computer presentation, perhaps linking to a ceiling-mounted projector that enables optimum flexibility in relaying your message. The general consensus is that a mainline presentation, individually prepared with back-up visuals where necessary, supported by a white board for explaining intricate detail, if required, is the most satisfactory way of getting your message across.

The key issues with regard to visuals are: Do not use too many different types in one presentation; only use keywords if absolutely necessary; please remember the content; and check the sequence! And remember that your visuals compete with you as regards your message to the audience. Having said that, however, Thomas J. Watson said in 1910, 'I have found in listening to countless sales presentations, people remember 25 per cent of what they see, 25 per cent of what they hear and 75 per cent of what they see and hear'. As you can probably gather, nothing has changed in sales training!

Mannerisms

Mannerisms are important if people notice them. Jingling coins around in the pocket becomes distractive, fiddling with spectacles, jewellery, pens or watches also becomes a noticeable irritation. Using a pointer and starting to 'conduct the orchestra' can destroy your presentation. Walking about can be all right if your message is what one can describe as 'mobile'. There was an instance of a Professor of Chemistry, at Kings College London, who would lecture for maybe an hour stepping carefully over his briefcase, backwards and forwards. One of his students took the case away during the coffee break and the Professor continued to step over the 'case'. It transpired that, unfortunately, he had a bad leg, but this could not be construed as a mannerism!

The most common mannerism, apart from the physical ones, is the use of repetitive words. The IT industry is notorious for someone returning from a business meeting abroad, to bring back the 'word of the month'. I have known such words to be, for example, 'concomitant' – it means at the same time. If a presenter says 'at the same time' on several occasions no one will notice, but try concomitant! Presenters sometimes introduce obscure words as a means of showing superiority to the audience. Just try it and see what happens to the achievement of your objective! Finally, if you have any mannerisms, ask your colleagues to point them out to you. It is better that they tell you that you are scratching your left ear, with your right hand behind your head while presenting, than losing a commitment!

Conclusion

As mentioned before, this can be the difficult bit. Hopefully you will have reached the point in your presentation where you can say, 'Ladies and gentlemen, based upon the cost-justified business case we have jointly produced, may I have your approval to proceed?' If the answer is yes – congratulations, but if the answer is something else then we need to find out what we actually have achieved and what we need to do next. This is the part that requires improvisation. The first thing to do is to agree with the audience what actually has been confirmed. From that you can produce a net list of outstanding issues. With this list, upon which you must obtain agreement there and then, that it *is* all that is preventing you from going ahead with the order, clearly state precisely what you will do next, with timescales. If appropriate, agree with the user what they should do next. Then, obtain a conditional agreement that if all issues are satisfactorily involved on both sides then approval will be granted. There is a lot more to this subject, but suffice it to say at this time, end *confidently* – with a bang, not a whimper. Remember that the audience will take in your final message. Don't come up with something gimmicky like 'You will be safe with this solution – you know it makes sense!' Say something more along the lines of 'I am confident that we can resolve these issues to your complete satisfaction and I very much look forward to the opportunity of working with you to bring the implementation to a successful conclusion'.

SUMMARY

With regard to user presentations, try to present your written proposals as often as you possibly can. Do not rely upon the written document to do the selling for you. If necessary, marshal supporting resources to accompany you at the presentation, for example your line manager or support manager (if appropriate, according to level of audience). Spend as long as is necessary to produce a really faultless piece of work and do not forget that your 'customer'-to-be knows more about their business than you do! Avoid any form of familiarity during the presentation and relax as your audience relaxes. Media distortion can affect communication; if you are over-confident, they will be suspicious. If you are nervous, they will be even more so. Try to strike a realistic balance, and come over as a professional who has done it before!

OUTSOURCING TRAINING

Finally, there is the question of using external training companies. The obvious downside is cost, as good courses invariably have a significant price tag associated with them. However, external trainers do have a number of advantages:

1. They will be experts in their field and therefore will be able to pass on real knowledge to the talented employee.

2. They will be up-to-date in their specialist field.

3. They will have learned from dealing with many organizations and can therefore deliver 'best practice'.

4. If they have been established for any length of time they will be expert at keeping staff motivated throughout a course.

Therefore the majority of companies do deem it appropriate to use external trainers occasionally and we would argue that this should apply particularly to those on a talent management fast-track programme.

CASE STUDIES

CASE STUDY 1: MAINTAINING AGGRESSIVE GROWTH PLANS THROUGHOUT EUROPE

The situation

A US software company wished to maintain its aggressive growth plans throughout Europe and Scandinavia. This was getting harder to achieve as other US companies were beginning to compete for market share. It was also introducing a new product which necessitated selling to the chief executive in the client organization, as opposed to its previous product range that was sold primarily to finance directors or controllers.

Key issues

The company wanted to undertake training for all its customer-facing staff throughout Europe and Scandinavia, to both enhance the general level of sales and account management skills and to focus on what new approaches and skill sets would be necessary to sell the new product. It also wanted to identify the most talented of its staff in the different countries, which was particularly relevant as many of them were new to the company, having been recruited to achieve the growth plans.

Problems to overcome

At one time the company had invested significantly in its in-house sales training capability. Over a period of years this had suffered through a lack of investment leading to an acknowledgement that the current trainers were mediocre. It was considered that they would not be capable of doing justice to the training requirements identified. It was also recognized that the trainers had no knowledge of the new skills required to sell the new product to the chief executive and other members of the board.

The solution

The software company had been approached by a partner in a leading sales and management training company that by coincidence had been an employee of the software company some years before. In addition to having had a successful sales and management career in that software company he had gone on to become the sales director of a company selling solutions similar to its new product, to chief executives. Following that he had been delivering sales and management training to many leading IT companies in the UK.

Based on his first-hand knowledge of the software company, and his experience with its competitors, he was able to tailor the training company's sales modules to fit precisely the training requirements. This involved the development of realistic example case studies, one for each country, which allowed the participants to practise their sales approach in general and specifically for the new product.

The process involved developing a general approach to the new product sales with senior managers based in the UK and this approach was then taken to each country manager for discussion and amendment. In particular, the different ways in which top executives worked in the different countries were analysed and each country manager helped to develop the accepted sales approach for the new product. These differences included hours of working, degrees of formality expected, the use of networks to gain access and the use of the software company's own senior management in the sales process.

The course also had to introduce the salespeople to the buying motivations of the chief executive and other board members as in the past the majority of sales had been made only to finance departments.

Prior to attending the course, each participant undertook the sales knowledge assessment and the results were used by the trainer to ascertain where precisely to pitch the material for the different competencies identified.

During each course the trainer carefully observed each attendee and noted how they contributed to group sessions, how they worked in their teams and how well they performed during the role-plays relating to the detailed case study.

Based on all this input the trainer submitted a written report on each candidate to both the local manager and to the European Vice President based in London. This report identified strengths and weaknesses observed from the sales knowledge assessment results and behaviour on the course as identified above.

To increase the opportunity for both learning and feedback, the role-plays were videotaped and provided to the local country managers for later review with the participants. The local managers were also encouraged to go through the trainer's report with each participant and to agree what additional training was required to address any shortfalls identified. The reports were also provided to the European Vice President to assist with the talent management aspect of the programme.

Outcome and benefits achieved

Courses were run in England, Scotland, France, Germany, Italy, Spain, Holland, Belgium, Norway, Sweden and Denmark.

The participants all received consistent messages on both general sales and account management techniques as well as product-specific strategies adapted to suit each country's business practices.

The country managers were enthusiastic about the training as it was skill enhancing and motivational. In addition, they received an objective appraisal of each of their staff in relation to sales ability.

The European Vice President was able to identify talented individuals with the most potential whom he fast tracked into more senior roles either within their own country's organization or by appointing them to posts in other countries.

The company continued to hit its impressive growth targets over the next three years.

Reinforcement programme to prevent future recurrence

Having realized that it had under-invested in sales training in the past, the software company retained the sales and management training company to develop and run a series of sales training courses over a period of three years. These covered introductory, intermediate and advanced selling techniques and account development skills. Each customer-facing employee went through the whole programme with the result that at the end of the three-year period there was a strong and consistent sales culture throughout the European part of the company.

CHAPTER 6

Performance Appraisal

WHY ARE MANY PERFORMANCE APPRAISAL SYSTEMS LESS THAN EFFECTIVE?

There have been many books written on the subject of performance appraisal and they describe the processes involved in great detail. In theory, at least, the concepts are very sound but, in practice, a number of operational problems emerge, mostly regarding non-standardized approaches to managing the appraisal preparation, approval procedures and execution of the interviews themselves.

The purpose of this work is not to outline the structures of the methods that have already been put into practice (which, in the main, are well known to most managers) but to highlight the limitations and associated problems. The objective here will be to look at better ways of ensuring consistency in a talent management programme.

First of all, formal appraisal systems, experienced by many people, have some serious drawbacks. Some of those are outlined below:

- Managers preparing appraisal interviews sometime have difficulty in completing the necessary paperwork in time for the interview which might well have been scheduled by HR, due to work pressures and dealing with daily operational issues.

- In some cases, unfortunately, the interviewing manager might take an 'easy' option and rate a subordinate higher than their actual performance achievement to save time and avoid any unpleasant confrontations. This can be compared with the erstwhile bank manager who said 'yes' to an overdraft rather than 'no' because 'yes' took five minutes and 'no' – 45 minutes!

- In some cases, a first-line manager may have too many people reporting in, which makes it difficult to really have an insight into the exact value of the subordinate's performance.

- Occasionally, a line manager could 'mark down' a talented subordinate's performance for fear of releasing them to another part of the business, thereby losing a valuable resource.

- It is all too easy for the interviewing manager to appear as 'the judge' rather than as a counsellor prepared to help the subordinate develop further.

- There is also the matter of favouring a subordinate whom the manager has identified as being the 'natural successor' so that the manager's next move might be accelerated.

There are other factors that can affect a realistic appraisal, but the above should provide a core of common problems associated with this process. If any reader finds the above observations to be difficult to comprehend, they can be assured that the world of big business is riddled with such examples. The conclusion that can be gained on the basis of a one-to-one appraisal process is that it can be very effective but human frailty can, and often does, affect objectivity.

AN OVERVIEW OF PERFORMANCE APPRAISAL TECHNIQUES

Some appraisal methods are well known; others less well known by title, perhaps, but are used by many organizations under different labels.

Let us have a brief look at some of the methods used. One of the best-known concepts is management by objectives (MBO).

This was originally conceived as an approach to encourage employees to work in close collaboration with their management, jointly to develop a set of mutually agreed objectives that could be realistically achieved in a planned timescale. Although MBO has undoubted merits, the main problem associated with it is that managers appear to take into account the employee's input but in the final analysis, tend to set the objectives the way in which they planned to do in the first place! This is particularly common in the case of junior employees who need 'guidance'.

DIARY APPRAISAL

This approach requires that a line manager maintain a record of positive and negative incidents, faithfully recorded by date and subject for review with the employee concerned during a one-to-one appraisal interview. It immediately springs to mind that there could be a highly subjective set of 'goods and bads' that might take some considerable elapsed time to be aired. Why wait for maybe several months to give an individual praise – 'Well done in handling that mobilization issue in Project X' – and by a similar token in a negative situation 'You were late in March, June and September regarding the submission of your team highlight report'.

QUANTITATIVE AND QUALITATIVE APPRAISAL AND COUNSELLING

A large number of companies use this method. It consists essentially of three main documents:

a) *Employee input form* – designed to allow the employee to prepare some input into the appraisal process – for example, achievements, issues, concerns, career ambition, self-appraisal of performance and so on.

b) *Manager's appraisal form* – this will bring forward the objectives set at the previous appraisal (if appropriate) and a quantitative evaluation of the manager's assessment as to how well the objectives have been achieved. This is normally on the basis of something like the following:

1. Excellent: The employee has far exceeded the standards expected in all aspects of the role and delivered an exceptional performance.

2. Good: Overall expectations have been met and, in some cases, exceeded.

3. Just meets requirements: A generally satisfactory performance with few or no outstanding characteristics.

4. Unsatisfactory: The overall performance level has failed to meet expectations.

For each of the categories that the appraisal covers, the manager will also write a narrative justifying the input to the quantitative results. In addition, there will be an overall rating along the lines of the evaluation guidelines above, clearly the desired result being at least a 2-rating and in the case of a talent management programme, a 1-rating. Finally, the interviewing manager will prepare an outline of the next period's objectives.

c) *Superior manager's approval* – no such appraisal will be deemed valid unless the manager's manager signs off the pre-interview documentation. The reasons for this should be self-evident.

THE INTERVIEW

Generally, this will be scheduled well in advance, in line with HR 'prompting', and the date committed, only to be changed in exceptional circumstances. Typically a good interview can last a couple of hours or more, to provide a forum for complete and frank interchange of ideas and views. At the conclusion of the interview, when all objectives for the future have been accepted (or, in some case, otherwise) the documentation, signed by the employee and the interviewing manager, with any endorsements (normally submitted by the employee), are returned to the superior manager for final approval and registration with the HR department.

This appears to be a very sensible approach to constructive appraisals.

FIELD OBSERVATION AND REVIEW

In the case of field personnel, such as salespeople, customer support personnel and field engineers, appraisals are often based upon performance in customers' offices. The accompanying manager closely assesses the performance of the employee. There then starts a process by which the employee is debriefed by what is known as 'kerbside counselling'. In practice, the employee and the manager return to the car to review what has been achieved and what might have been improved. The manager records the discussion and sends a copy to the employee for monitoring areas for improvement and input to, say, a periodic review together with a 'collection' of such records. The limiting factor here is that the reviews still rely upon the opinions of the supervising manager, or at best, those of the superior manager in addition, who will not be personally familiar with the events recorded.

There are some other methods traditionally used but they all have similar limitations to those outlined above. Let us now look at a more sophisticated form of appraisal known as 360-degree assessment.

360-DEGREE ASSESSMENT

This transcends the limitations of just one-to one appraisal and uses input from the various people with whom the employee interfaces. This might involve all or some of the following:

- superior manager
- peer groups

- internal staff groups

- internal 'customers'

- external customers

- subordinates

- senior management.

This is shown in Figure 6.1.

It has been demonstrated that using multiple inputs, as above, provides a far more accurate measurement of an employee's effectiveness. This is because, amongst other things, a global view of all those people who deal with the employee is likely to be far more comprehensive and objectively balanced, rather than the opinion gained from a one-to-one assessment.

We can now begin to see how valuable this concept could be in a talent management environment where excellence needs to be recognized by a wide variety of people, both internally and externally.

However, the situation is not quite so straightforward. There are a number of factors to be considered as follows:

- the company's education programme

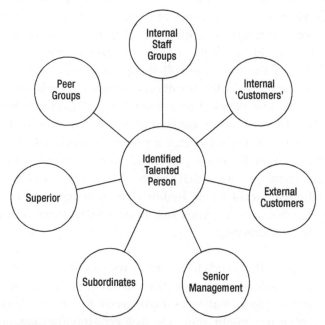

Figure 6.1   360-degree assessment

- its strategic mission

- its culture and 'personality'.

This essentially means that the type and source of feedback must be carefully sought and compiled in line with the policies and practices of the company, particularly when using external sources of assessment. An example of this might be where a customer makes a critical appraisal, either internal or external, based upon the employee's inability to accede to a request that is not part of permitted practice.

There are some real advantages, however. What better to have positive feedback from peer groups with regard to the employee's capability in teamwork? Or the satisfaction of a user who has managed to achieve all the results and objectives claimed prior to a project being implemented?

Consider another factor. As the employee is also part of this 360-degree assessment, an assessment of the management performance can provide valuable input into style, technique and effectiveness.

It now becomes clear that a plan for 360-degree assessment must be formulated specifically for each job type and employee. Equally as important, diagnosing the additional knowledge required to fill the gaps revealed by knowledge assessment means that the next vital action is to ensure that the necessary development programmes are put into place and then designed around a reinforcement process to maximize the effect of the required changes. In practice this would normally indicate regular review and monitoring of progress. One of the more difficult things to achieve in any training or development programme is the retention of trained knowledge. In view of this, it is advisable that people taking knowledge assessments are informed in advance that they will be re-assessed after, say, six months. In that way, people are conditioned to the fact that it was not a simple case of just taking an assessment and attendance at a prescribed training course. Quite often, the view taken is, 'Thank goodness that's over – let's get back to the real world!' Well, this is the real world where highly accurate diagnosis has been made of areas for improvement in which significant progress can be made under carefully planned conditions.

There is one point that needs to be considered carefully: does the candidate need to take the whole assessment again, including the categories that were satisfactory, or just those that were highlighted for improvement? In the main, most authorities might conclude that post-training assessment need only concentrate upon those priorities earlier diagnosed. This ability to assess performance improvement allows for repeated feedback.

WHAT ARE THE BENEFITS OF THIS CONCEPT?

First of all, if properly administrated, the company gets people who are motivated to improve and secondly, any reinforcement and monitoring procedures provide up-to-date real-time feedback.

So far, we have considered using knowledge assessment as the basis of improvement but there is also the very important contribution that psychometric assessment can make to ensure that behavioural issues can be addressed, if necessary. If managers can be empowered to measure behavioural tendencies, and concentrate upon helping employees to put those which detract from optimum performance in place, the most likely outcome is going to be a much more knowledgeable and polished professional – just what is needed for serious talent management.

One thing is for sure, when we consider the amount of money that is spent on training budgets, some of it, unfortunately, is wasted; how much better would it be to make the point of training people in what they need to know, rather than what they already know, or worse, what they do not need to know as far as their current or known future assignments are concerned?

It has been said that using 360-degree assessment properly for validating performance improvement is a major contributor to effective talent management.

PERFORMANCE APPRAISAL AND FUTURE PERFORMANCE

One frequent criticism of performance appraisals is their focus on past performance. Most of the assessment process is based on how the individual performed in the review period against established targets or behavioural objectives. Relatively little attention is paid to the future development of the individual being assessed.

Where deficiencies in skill, knowledge or performance are identified, it is important to discuss how these can be remedied.

The performance appraisal process should, therefore, provide the opportunity for the person being assessed to identify areas where they feel that training is required in order to help them improve their future performance.

By shifting the focus from past performance to future improvement, the appraisal process is likely to achieve a higher level of internal acceptance.

In order to demonstrate that the issue is treated seriously, there needs to be an element within the appraisal process that considers the impact of training received in terms of both knowledge levels and changes in performance.

The following is a recommended approach:

- competency area – the aspect of capability or skill that is being appraised

- assessed score – the rating given at the previous assessment

- recommended training – the identified course or training programme that will be used to improve performance

- pre-training KA – the knowledge assessment of the individual prior to attendance on the course

- training undertaken – the record of the course(s) attended

- post-training KA – the rating achieved from the knowledge assessment conducted after the training has been completed (training impact assessment)

- current assessment – the competency rating achieved at the current performance appraisal.

This process demonstrates that the company has a serious interest in helping employees improve their individual knowledge levels and performance potential.

One interesting dimension is the conduct of the knowledge assessment pre- and post- the training programme. Training impact analysis is an important element in managing the training budget and in identifying which training techniques deliver the best results.

Another dimension is the requirement for the assessor to identify suitable training programmes so that the HR department is able to provide a comprehensive catalogue of internal and external courses. It is fairly common in this process to identify training needs where existing courses do not exist and this can be a useful input to the scope of the training programme.

PERFORMANCE APPRAISAL AND TALENT MANAGEMENT

Within the context of talent management strategy, the performance appraisal process needs to consider a further dimension – future potential. The basic question is 'how high can this individual go?'

The performance appraisal is, therefore, not only an assessment of performance in the appraisal period but also an appraisal of future potential based upon historical performance.

This is likely to introduce an element of career planning in terms of assignments designed to either test capabilities or broaden experience.

In some organizations there is a deliberate policy of moving high achievers between line and staff functions and between head office and regional operations. The appraisal process should, therefore, include an evaluation of available opportunities or needs and the identification of suitable appointments.

Judgements as to the ultimate potential of an individual are likely to change over time and so it is important to consider how previous predictions may have changed on the basis of the current appraisal.

The ultimate potential assessment should also include a timeline. This is a valuable input into the succession planning process and may include such observations as:

Ultimate potential:	Executive Director
Timescale:	5–7 years
Intermediate potential:	Divisional Director
Timescale:	1–2 years
Current role:	Regional Manager

These observations would need to be accompanied by recommendations for specific training in order to prepare the individual for the intermediate role.

From experience, performance appraisals of senior staff introduce a further dimension which relates to business or operational issues. Their inputs are likely to be a rich source of information on how the organization is performing and where improvements could be made.

Accordingly, it is useful to broaden the scope of the appraisal to include specific questions on operational experience in the current function and how it could be improved.

COACHES AND MENTORS

We have already identified the roles of coaches and mentors within the talent management strategy.

Where they exist, their inputs should form part of the appraisal process. The coach should be able to comment on how the individual has been able to master the requirements of the incumbent role, while the mentor should comment on overall performance, potential and development objectives.

Both coaches and mentors may also provide valuable inputs to the ultimate potential assessment and suitability for intermediate roles.

CASE STUDY

CASE STUDY 1: HOW TO DEVELOP TALENT FROM AN EXISTING FIELD FORCE BY PRODUCT ORIENTATED SALES TRAINING (POST) INVOLVING THOROUGH PERFORMANCE REVIEW

Situation

An international telecommunications company became concerned about the level of productivity of its apparently elite and talented field force. The hit rate for orders from direct sales, on average, was one in six; in other words, for every six proposals submitted, only one order was gained. One further order went to competition, but four decided to do nothing – well below industry sales standards for the offerings in question. In other words, less than 17 per cent of sales effort was productive and the remaining 83 per cent wasted.

Initial assessments had revealed that its support people, systems engineers and consultants, were highly knowledgeable regarding product capability and the sales force was highly motivated and generally very capable in terms of the knowledge, skill and behavioural attitudes required to recognize a business opportunity, seize it and bring it to a conclusion by way of a signed contract.

However, further investigation of capability showed that the support people needed more business awareness and the sales force needed to understand not only the products but more importantly, product capability. After all, people do not just buy 5 mm drills; they buy 5 mm holes!

The company had a range of some seven major products, from simple base systems and handsets to complex switches used by larger organizations.

The salespeople and support personnel were assigned to teams providing a total customer field sales and support service by individual product specialization. The position as perceived by the company was that support personnel needed more knowledge of sales processes and sales needed to become more total solution-aware involving the ability to translate product capability into irresistible solutions that the customer would readily understand and buy.

Key issues

The most pressing problem was how to design a programme to provide all that was necessary for the support people to be able to assess the sales and buying cycles, while, at the same time, provide the salespeople with sufficient knowledge of product and applications know-how to be as self-sufficient as possible in the early stages of the sales process. Furthermore, in order to conserve resources, the subject of prospect qualification became a discipline to both sales and support, the latter being in a position to police the sales function where insufficient verification of a realistic sales situation had been identified.

In addition to this, the company acknowledged that they probably had a highly talented field force but perhaps not all the talent had been realized in many areas.

Problems to overcome

- How to balance the training needs of both sales and support personnel?

- Should the training be application or product oriented?

- Would different training materials be required for sales and support?

- What form should the training take?

- Should they capitalize on the team/product concept or try a different approach?

- How would performance before, during and after the training be effectively measured?

The solution

The concept of POST (Product Oriented Sales Training) was established with case studies interspersed with theory sessions and role-plays. These were not only taken by trainers and line managers but also suitably qualified customer personnel at various levels were invited to attend and evaluate intermediate and final presentations. This served to provide as realistic a forum as possible to encourage all field personnel, both sales and support, to experience customer reaction plus the intensive review of their performances by internal management.

Typically, each workshop lasted three or five days, depending on the complexity of the offering.

An agenda would have included the following items, amongst others:

- introduction, aims and objectives
- process of performance measurement
- why do we win or lose business?
- the importance of qualification
- how the best sales teams operate
- major case study – industry and product oriented
- objection handling clinic
- presenting a proposal for change
- closing technique.

The major case study would be specially written to reflect the product capability needed within the target market or industry and would reflect the corresponding theory sessions to ensure that participants really understood the key issues involved in solving customer needs.

One of the essential features of the process was the performance review carried out at every stage of the case study development. Every role-play call was reviewed by a panel of assessors comprising trainers, line managers, staff managers, for example legal, finance, marketing and business practices, plus the appropriate customer representative to award a rating based upon the following formula:

- excellent – near perfect

- very good – made substantial progress

- good – sale has progressed

- neutral – no measurable advancement

- unsatisfactory.

The 'panel' assessing each call needed to agree much the same as a jury and as soon as conclusions were reached, they were communicated to the participant(s) in the form of personal interviews.

In practice, each participant was measured over a series of nine such exercises and a picture of their progress was built up as the workshop continued.

For talent management purposes, the company sought 4–5 excellents and 4–5 very goods in order to gain access to the about-to-be-announced talent programme.

Outcome and benefits achieved

The results of the training were very interesting.

The number of people involved in the initial training was as follows:

Salespeople	All products	452
Support personnel	All products	232
Consultants	All products	37

Those who met the stringent qualification criteria were:

Salespeople	108
Support	41
Consultants	15

This exercise illustrated that 24 per cent of salespeople met the talent standards, 4 per cent higher than the norm.

Only 18 per cent of support personnel met or exceeded the required standard, 2 per cent below par, and 40 per cent of consultants were successful. The best thing that the company could have done was to isolate their best people and concentrate on continuing their talent development over a carefully planned period to ensure that their contribution to the company's future welfare was in the best hands.

Having determined the talent base, the company had established those criteria that could be set as new standards for recruitment and development. The only question remaining is what was to be done with the lower-level performers?

Reinforcement programme to prevent future recurrence

The first conclusion reached was that real talent needed to be assessed in advance, not in retrospect. Secondly, the recruitment process to identify such talent would need to be matched against the profiles of existing outstanding performers.

Just identifying talent in the future would not guarantee a consistent development process unless matched by a talent advancement programme in conjunction with an ongoing assessment mechanism designed to ensure that previously identified talented people would be capable of assuming the increasing responsibilities of more complex assignments.

The real lesson that was learned was – do not just assume talent will develop on its own. It has to be nurtured.

CHAPTER 7

The IT Infrastructure

INTRODUCTION

Organizations running talent management programmes will almost certainly have a formal programme through which selected staff will attend various modules designed to provide a thorough all-round knowledge of the company and its key functions. It is unlikely that the progress of staff through such programmes can be monitored effectively either at the individual or programme level without implementing an effective IT system. Moreover, the key to a really successful talent management system revolves around the ability to measure, very accurately, the benefits achieved and to be able to provide top management with a true statement regarding the return on the investment made in talent management.

Unfortunately, many people have, in the recent past, regarded talent management as a cost, albeit a desirable process but not necessarily a business investment. An automated system can go a long way in not only collecting and compiling data but also assist in handling the talent characteristics of large numbers of people.

Most large organizations have programmes for succession planning in place for their most senior people but a properly structured talent management system goes much further and allows monitoring of talent much further down into the company, thus allowing the organization to cater for its key people at many levels.

One word of caution, however: before thinking about constructing a database, it very important to define, very clearly, the existing and planned requirements of the talent structure in terms of the areas to be covered. Further thought should also be given to catering for change and additions in line with the future needs of the business. For example, do we know the scope of our performance management systems or competency frameworks? What is likely to be the resultant effect of organic or acquisition growth? Sound planning of short-, medium- and long-term requirements will certainly be a contributing effect to the success of the automated system.

If you are planning to get deeply involved in a talent management programme, then perhaps you ought also to consider a training management system to work alongside it. Not only would you then be able to plan training events based upon individual and group requirements but the system could be used to approve the courses, make the bookings, take care of billing for external courses and monitor results for delivery to the right quarters.

Some systems that are available today even manage the administration of all types of courses, web-based distance learning, outsourced training events and even training designed to help the individual dynamically on the job. Others have the provision for creating first-class visual and audio support for newly designed events. Furthermore, the analysis available from such systems is extremely valuable to everyone involved in the training circuit. No longer is it necessary for HR to have to remind line managers to send people on a course. The system does all that automatically. The scope can be expanded even further. Not only does the administration of the training function become streamlined, it can also be linked to performance appraisal systems to tie in with the talent management programme.

In this regard, it is important to consider that talent management and training administration need to be equally catered for. Talented people become very disillusioned if they feel that their training and development needs are not being covered properly and, unfortunately, many talented people have left their employer to seek an alternative where training needs were sensitively handled.

Information technology, if properly conceived, is capable of providing a wealth of management information, particularly in helping to measure the level of return on the investment that would have been made. This is true to some extent wherever IT is used, but it is equally relevant to the question of talent management investment.

Another important benefit falls within the HR function. Because a great deal of drudgery is removed involving perhaps quite a large overhead, HR becomes much more effective and recognized as being able to provide top management within the company with data upon which personal development decisions can be made with far more confidence.

Some companies decide to purchase commercially available systems rather than build their own. There can be much merit in this, provided that certain precautionary measures are considered.

The first issue is to establish whether suppliers can actually provide the level of information through their systems that top management need. Then there is the problem of issues other than functionality, that is, support, maintenance and training for users.

Another development that has taken place is the reorientation of HR since the early days of the personnel department. Their influence has increased substantially with easy access to top management but, not only that, budgets that used to sit primarily in IT have more often than not been reallocated to HR for personnel data systems.

In many companies, HR can make procurement decisions for such acquisitions with or without the approval of IT. This may or may not be a satisfactory situation. As the main function of IT is to translate the operating and corporate needs of the company into a balanced IT strategy, any out-of-line hybrid solutions could affect the overall function of IT.

In any case, finance management should always be involved in serious expenditure and they would perhaps seek concurrence from IT to ensure that any proposed move is 'inside the plan'.

One of the reasons for this shift has been the acknowledgement of top management of the need for effective talent programmes as an investment opportunity and, of course, managers outside of the purchasing department are more frequently making decisions on procurement processes.

However, HR, with their increased involvement in supplier relationships, have proved to be tough buyers in many cases. They will typically demand justification for return on investment and case studies, supported by reference information, which they will follow up to verify claims made by suppliers.

Purchasing ready-made systems, even those that appear to provide the specification needed, cannot always replace the system needs of a dynamic and fast-growing organization.

There are a number of situations that need to be carefully considered:

- Does the supplier provide adequate support for an international or multinational company? This point has to be thought out very carefully for two quite different reasons. The first is that if a talent management system is to be run as a global entity, there must be a common business language used throughout. If HQ is receiving input from overseas subsidiaries, there is hardly any point in the HR department in the subsidiary only operating in the local language, as the input would be difficult to use. The second point is that terminology throughout the organization needs to be standardized, in addition to the language itself.

- Will the people be able to use the system easily without a high level of system awareness?

- Can all systems in the international network be properly co-ordinated and supported by the supplier, with particular reference to making system changes that would affect the entire operation?

If a combined talent management programme and training management system are to be undertaken, we believe that at least the talent portion should be built internally.

It needs to be managed as a critical project involving HR, finance, line management and the project team, orchestrated by a relationship manager who would be totally familiar with the business and technical requirements. It clearly requires the absolute commitment and support of top management.

We hope the following will provide some basic guidelines in initiating such an approach.

This Chapter seeks to set out a broad outline of a possible database structure for a talent management IT system, which allows an individual's progress to be planned and monitored, and for management reports to be produced. The structure is not intended as a complete prescription but is meant to provide a starting point for organizations to amend and use in the light of their specific requirements.

THE DATABASE STRUCTURE

The database consists of seven tables:

1. *Person* – this table holds the basic details of each person who is taking part in the talent management programme.

2. *Individual programme* – each person in the talent management programme will have one entry in this table to detail the planned movement and timescales for their particular assignments throughout the organization. This individual programme is defined at entry to the talent management programme.

3. *Positions* – keeps a history of the positions in the organization held by a person in the talent management programme.

4. *Assessments* – keeps a record of all the knowledge assessments taken by a person in the talent management programme.

5. *Qualifications* – holds the academic and other qualifications gained by each person.

6. *Psychometrics* – keeps a record of the results of the psychometric assessments taken by a person.

7. *Mentors* – holds the details of the mentor assigned to each person in the talent management programme.

Figure 7.1 shows the tables and the relationships between them; it can be seen that the most important table is the Person table and this is linked to all the tables except the Mentors table by the personal ID of the participant. Typically this personal ID will be the number or identifying code assigned when the employee joins the company, so it will be unique to them. The mentor ID can either be the mentor's company ID or an identifier generated by the database itself.

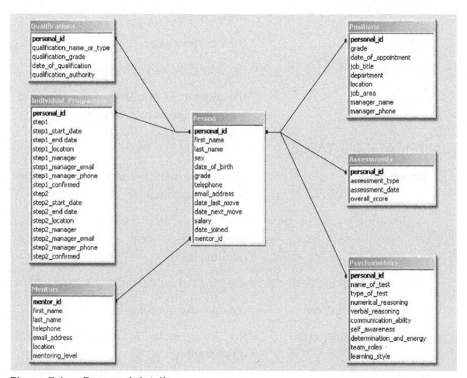

Figure 7.1   Personal details

PERSON TABLE

personal_id	the unique identifier in the organization for this staff member
first_name	the person's first name
last_name	the person's last name
sex	their sex – while not directly relevant for talent management this is useful for statistical purposes
date_of_birth	date of birth
grade	current grade in the organization
telephone	internal contact number
email address	internal email address
date_last_move	the date of the last move within the organization
date_next_move	the date of the next move within the organization
salary	their current salary
date_joined	the date they joined the organization
mentor_id	the mentor_id pointing to the allocated mentor in the Mentors table

QUALIFICATIONS TABLE

personal_id	the unique identifier in the organization for this staff member
qualification_name_or_type	the name or type of academic, professional or other relevant qualification
qualification_grade	the grade of qualification attained
date_of_qualification	the date the qualification was attained
qualification_authority	the organization issuing the qualification

ASSESSMENTS TABLE

personal_id	the unique identifier in the organization for this staff member
assessment_type	the type of assessment taken
assessment_date	the date the assessment was taken
overall_score	the overall score attained in the assessment

POSITIONS TABLE

personal_id	the unique identifier in the organization for this staff member
grade	the grade while in this position
date_of_appointment	that date on which the appointment was made
job_title	the title of the position
department	the name of the department
location	where the position is based
job_area	the type of work carried out
manager_name	the name of the direct manager for this position
manager_phone	the manager's phone number

PSYCHOMETRICS TABLE

personal_id	the unique identifier in the organization for this staff member
name_of_test	the name of the test taken
type_of_test	which area of behaviour the test covers
numerical_reasoning	from SHL's Ability Screening Online
verbal_reasoning	from SHL's Ability Screening Online
communication_ability	from Myers-Briggs Indicators

self_awareness	based on the output from the FIRO-B® questionnaire
determination_and_energy	from the SHL OPQ32 test
team_roles	the preferred team roles from Belbin's assessment
learning_style	from the Honey and Mumford questionnaire

MENTORS TABLE

mentor_id	the unique identifier in the organization for this mentor
first_name	the mentor's first name
last_name	the mentor's last name
telephone	internal contact number
email_address	internal email address
location	where the mentor is based
mentoring_level	an indication of the mentoring expertise for this mentor

INDIVIDUAL PROGRAMME TABLE

The number of steps in a programme will usually be between seven and ten; two steps are shown just to indicate the replication of fields.

personal_id	the unique identifier in the organization for this staff member
step1	the type/name of the function
step1_start_date	the date the step should be started
step1_end_date	the date the step should be ended
step1_manager	the responsible manager for this step; this is the name of the manager responsible for talent management in this department
step1_manager_email	the step manager's email address

step1_manager_phone	the step manager's phone number
step2	the type/name of the function
step2_start_date	the date the step should be started
step2_end_date	the date the step should be ended
step2_manager	the responsible manager for this step; this is the name of the manager responsible for talent management in this department
step2_manager_email	the step manager's email address
step2_manager_phone	the step manager's phone number

REPORTS

Each organization will need to generate its own set of reports tailored to its requirements but these typically fall into two distinct categories: those used to manage an individual in the programme and those used to monitor the overall programme.

At the individual level it is important to be able to check that they are making the required progress and this is not being hindered either by lack of sufficient training or organizational problems.

A typical individual report might contain the following items where the use of assessments and reviews has assigned a numeric value to each item:

- strategy – understanding current status and planning future activity

- change management – recognizing the need for change and ensuring everyone likely to be affected is involved, providing input and reinforcement of change procedures

- time management – prioritizing tasks to manage time in a structured manner

- decision-making processes – how decisions are made; the process and key people involved

- decision criteria – the basis upon which decisions are to be made, for example timescale, choice of methodology and so on

- success track record – the record of successful completion of tasks and assignments

- business case development – preparing a value proposition document for a new assignment

- communication skills – internal and external communication capability including presentations

- teamwork – working as an integral part of a developed or undeveloped team

- conflict management – managing both healthy and unhealthy conflict internally (and externally, if appropriate)

- allocation of resources – managing people and facilities

- interpersonal skills – dealing with superiors, subordinates, peer groups, staff groups, external suppliers and contractors

- IT awareness – dealing with superiors, subordinates, peer groups, staff groups, external suppliers and contractors

- motivation – ability to demonstrate self-sufficiency in day-to-day IT methods and adopting new methodologies

- budgetary control – managing any assigned financial budgets.

If the output from this report is combined with the same report from other participants in the programme in a tabular form then averaged across the whole group, it is possible to assess the effectiveness of the programme in each of these areas (see Figure 7.2 which shows a subset of the suggested items).

If the acceptable score is 50 then it can be seen that the programme as a whole is achieving its objective for conflict, but George needs some extra help. On the other hand, in the part of the programme on change an average score of 44 with three participants achieving less than 50 indicates that there might be an issue in this area of the programme that needs to be addressed.

NAME	STRATEGY	CHANGE	COMMUNICATION	CONFLICT
JULIE CARR	65	47	55	70
JAMES HULME	55	35	67	59
GEORGE SMITH	72	51	52	41
FRANCIS BLUNDELL	78	42	61	53
OVERALL AVERAGE	67	44	59	56

Figure 7.2   Measurement factors

Figure 7.2 provides a simple illustration of the type of output that can be extracted from the database. We can go much further by extending the concept to show a comprehensive management information system that can be geared to top management requirements, HR controls and monitoring, and also provide valuable data to line and career managers who will need to gauge the effectiveness of the talent management administration.

Then there is the question of establishing analyses by individual, team, group and even the whole company to measure where corrective action, if any, needs to be taken. In a talent management operation, standards will inevitably be set higher than, say, the norms we saw in Chapter 4 relating to basic knowledge assessment. We can prioritize the importance of each of the subjects covered by the programme depending on the precise profile objectives of the individual and the job type.

For example, of the fifteen areas outlined on the previous page, it might well be that strategy, change management, communications and teamwork are classed as priority 'A' subjects and measured at a very high norm, say 80 per cent. This means that standards in these subjects will be carefully scrutinized to ensure that only the very best performers will proceed through the programme. By regular review, the parameters can be changed to match prevailing needs and to cater for a wide variety of statistics.

GROUP AND INDIVIDUAL ANALYSIS

GROUP REVIEWS

In Figure 7.3 we are examining a module completed by a particular group of people who were originally hired as graduate intakes but have now progressed to a higher management potential programme within the concept of talent management. They will all have completed a series of skill rehearsals, presentations, case studies and interviews by specially selected line and staff managers.

Threshold priorities have been set in accordance with the business requirements and are shown next to the category in question. Some of the priority settings are very high, requiring a level of excellence by the people in question. The level of information produced by the database completely removes any possibility of guesswork or subjective measurements. The analysis enables the person managing the programme participant to clearly explain why the results are as recorded. It is important to note that if a knowledge assessment has been used as part of this module, the interviewer can not only

TALENT MANAGEMENT MODULE 3
GROUP 3 ASSESSMENT

NAME	JOB LEVEL	STRATEGY 80%	BUSINESS CONTROLS 80%	CHANGE MANAGEMENT 75%	CONFLICT MANAGEMENT 85%	COMMUNICATION SKILL 85%	TEAMWORK 80%	RESOURCE USAGE 50%	NEGOTIATION SKILL 50%
MADDY JOSEPH	PROJECT MANAGER	68	84	83	90	90	79	43	85
ALEX DAVIS	SALES MANAGER	85	81	85	93	83	82	48	85
OSCAR FAIRFAX	BUSINESS DEVELOPMENT MANAGER	63	80	93	73	90	80	42	77
SUMMER CATE	BUSINESS DEVELOPMENT MANAGER	82	66	69	73	77	86	40	62
KATIE ALGELINA	PROGRAMME MANAGER	82	67	85	100	93	74	42	54
CLAIRE CHURCH	BUSINESS DEVELOPMENT MANAGER	86	80	61	86	89	78	49	69
JIM DOHERTY	ACCOUNT DIRECTOR	96	71	79	73	90	87	38	92
SARAH BROWNE	SENIOR SALES EXECUTIVE	86	69	74	87	70	79	41	45
TOM CARSON	BUSINESS DEVELOPMENT MANAGER	84	90	79	77	91	81	42	77
ADAM DALE	SALES MANAGER	91	54	77	90	97	86	46	69
JOHN REILLY	DEVELOPMENT MANAGER	95	88	76	63	77	87	44	69

Figure 7.3　Group analysis

pinpoint the areas for review but actually identify the comparison between actual answers provided by the participant and the expected answer. In this way, it helps people to correct mistakes for future improvement.

First of all, let's look at the overall 'shape' of the analysis from a group standpoint:

1.　Of the eleven participants, Strategy seems to be well understood apart from two people who are significantly below the required threshold score of 80 per cent.

2.　Business controls – five people are below the expected standard.

3.　Change management – slight improvement.

4.　Conflict management – some very high scores, three reasonably close and one at 63 per cent that needs immediate review.

5.　Communication skill – again a very high threshold score but achievement of this score by top-flight people is essential.

6.　Teamwork – only fine-tuning needed by the four participants who have not quite met requirements.

7.　Resource usage – an urgent investigation is needed to understand why all eleven participants failed in this subject, even though the priority is relatively low.

INDIVIDUAL REVIEWS

The first observation is that Alex Davis is virtually up to the very high standards established, as is Tom Carson.

Maddy Joseph needs a little help in Strategy but it still remains, however, that Resource Usage, generally, is a potentially serious matter as far as standards of productivity are required.

Oscar Scott-Fairfax also has failed to meet the high standard demanded in Strategy and is sufficiently below the standard in Conflict Management to warrant a detailed review.

Katie Angelina has a problem with Business Controls which needs to be reviewed carefully but the rest of the profile, apart from the common problem with Resource Usage, is OK.

Adam Dale has done very well, exceeding expectations in six of the eight areas but immediate review of his performance in Business Controls needs to take place.

At the other end of the scale, Sarah Browne has only 'passed' in two of the subjects, albeit with close results in two further areas, Change Management and Teamwork, and Summer Cate has exposures in five areas, four of which are priority subjects.

All the remaining individual performances follow a similar pattern. The important issue is that these results need to be looked into. Remember that we are talking about specially selected people on a talent management programme.

What can we glean from this? Have the priority levels been set too high? Have we got the right people on the programme? Can effective corrective action be taken in a workable timescale for those who have not met the required standard? Do we need to revise the subject mix?

Whatever conclusions can be reached, the most important thing is that we have access to the *right information*. A properly designed database can make the difference between, at worst, getting the wrong people or perpetuating mediocrity, rather than progressing talent and realizing the importance of placing the future of the company in the very best hands, based upon analysis and review of sustained monitoring of performance.

As a rule of thumb, if you take a sample of 12 employees, two (the talented) just get on with the pursuit of excellence, three may be in the wrong job or even company, and the remaining seven will perform as middle-of-the-road practitioners but will be unlikely to reach 'talent' status.

It is the top performers who we need in order to ensure the results we seek.

EXTENDED APPLICATIONS

INTEGRATED ASSESSMENT

In Chapters 3 and 4 we looked at psychometric testing and knowledge assessment. These are both elements of the ways in which a person can be assessed and probably represent about two-thirds of the complete profile. To this we need to add skill and experience, normally assessed by, say, interviews of various types coupled with their track record of success.

This can be represented by a simple formula, ASK: Attitude, Skill and Knowledge.

An illustration of this could be for a first-line manager who has undertaken a series of psychometric assessments and a relevant knowledge assessment. A series of interviews may have been held to verify the contents and claims of the CV and an analysis produced.

First of all, we need to access the database to establish the results as reported by all the assessors involved.

For example, we could rate a manager on a scale of 1–5 where 5 = excellent, 4 = very good, 3 = good, 2 = above average, 1 = average, illustrating a maximum rating of 125 for all three sections (5 x 5 x 5).

If we were to apply this formula for integrated assessment we might come up with the relationship shown in Figure 7.4.

Therefore, various conclusions can be inferred from this data.

If in the case of (a) Bill Lewis, he has an attitude level that is high, skill is at a similar level and knowledge is low, this means that effectiveness is limited. It indicates that Bill is very positive, possibly liked by all but actually does not have the technical knowledge to influence things and relies upon relationships rather than problem-solving and solution-generation provided perhaps by

NAME	TITLE	ATTITUDE	SKILL	KNOWLEDGE	EFFECTIVENESS
BILL LEWIS	PRODUCT MANAGER	4	4	2	32/125
TONY BLAKE	DEVELOPMENT MANAGER	1	4	4	16/125
JILL WEBSTER	FINANCE MANAGER	5	4	4	80/125

Figure 7.4   ASK interpretation

support personnel. By a similar token, if in the case of (b) Tony Blake's attitude is low but skill and knowledge are high, the net result still presents a problem. What this means essentially is that this person has the skill and knowledge to do the job but he might be difficult to manage, because of the attitude issue.

However, in the case of (c) Jill Webster, where all three factors are at a high level, we are beginning to identify possible future talent. This is the sort of balance that we should be looking for.

Clearly, recording the information on the database is vital to obtain accurate measurement but experience has shown that where this type of discipline is employed, hiring and promotion decisions become very much more reliable in order to attract, develop and retain the best people.

So, the message is: complete a thorough assessment, covering attitude, skill and knowledge in order to minimize the risk of hiring the wrong person, or promoting someone beyond their capability.

DETERMINING THE EFFECTIVENESS OF TRAINING

One of the most difficult things to achieve in any training environment is the retention by the trainee of the trained information. Many people, hopefully not those on a talent management programme, attend training courses and when they return to work, say, 'It was good, but I cannot wait to get back to the real world!'

The fact is that the training event should truly reflect the real world but, even more, the participants should appreciate that they will be reassessed after a prescribed interval to see how they have absorbed and assimilated the work they learned on the course.

In practice, imagine this scenario:

A participant on a talent management programme is assessed by the various methods outlined in this book, one of which will relate to the knowledge required to do the job that is a knowledge assessment. Take the case of this first-line manager who took a knowledge assessment to determine the required training needs (TNA). Let us say that three areas were highlighted for review – conflict management, teamwork and leadership.

The participant's Career Manager arranged attendance at a specific module designed to address these issues, based upon the same KA disciplines and maybe some associated modules such as communication and negotiation skills.

The participant in question did well on the course but the issue still remained – How could we be sure that this knowledge will last? First of all, the Career Manager set up a series of regular review interviews to discuss relevant experiences that the participant may have encountered in the field and asked for a (fairly) formal presentation of the issues in relation to the training course previously attended. It was further determined that the participant would re-take the knowledge assessment at a set date.

The original results from the participant's database were accessed and a revised higher score (uplift) was calculated to be applied to the expected results for the re-take.

These were communicated clearly to the participant. This had the effect of encouraging the participant to concentrate upon the need to meet the new challenge.

One of the facilities within the KA concept is the ability to randomize the questions in terms of sequence and mix to remove any suggestion of 'remembering the questions'. However, experience has shown that virtually all KA participants have very little detailed recall of the process and it can be reasonably assumed that a similar assessment will be taken to the first round of assessments.

This is where the database comes into its own. Previous assessments will, of course, have been recorded and results transmitted to the relevant people. Now we introduce the uplift norms and the comparisons not only become quantitatively of immediate benefit but also we can actually see, by interrogating the database information, how the questions relating to the issues concerned have been addressed in response to the training experience. A specially written piece of software, as a function of the database, can enable the reviewing manager to become an 'instant' counsellor. This is based upon whether or not the training has been effective from the database information that represents the actual answers. This, matched against the standards set, shows a comparison of actual versus 'hoped-for' answers.

As a result of this, the reviewing manager can determine the success or otherwise of the training event in terms of retained capability.

The important message in all this is that we are not talking about a three-day training event – 'thank God that's over' – but effectively a notional three- or even six-month 'course' with a further assessment at the end of it. This is designed to ensure that the course participant on the talent management programme is well aware of the process and will have absorbed the information and is committed to the prescribed improvements.

DETERMINING BEST OF BREED USING THE DATABASE

Within a talent management programme, there is positive value in identifying the really outstanding performers of all those engaged in the talent management process.

The concept is concerned with understanding why consistently top performers operate in a certain way and can be identified conclusively from performance characteristics as recorded on the database and by completing a detailed questionnaire that is subsequently merged into the database records.

The first issue is to extract results such as those recorded in Figure 7.3. The results of the people who have really excelled in all categories that have been monitored can be isolated and then they can be invited to participate in a specially designed questionnaire based upon their actual business function.

By way of illustration, let us have a look at an extract from a suitable questionnaire designed for a Relationship Manager, a senior business practitioner responsible for co-ordinating the needs of a business unit and the capability of a project team in a strategic programme for the company.

The key issues that might be addressed by way of example are:

- performance characteristics over the past two years (from the database)

- age, period with company, period of this assignment, background (academic and professional qualifications (from the database)

- activity ratios – personal time management achievements

- assistance provided by the company in terms of processes to generate the highest standards of business excellence

- personal formula for effective communication

- attitude to preparing and conducting productive meetings

- short- and longer-term training requirements with illustrations of potential improvement

- personal motivational factors – money? Job satisfaction? Promotional opportunities? Recognition? In what priority sequence?

- analysis of proven productive and unproductive procedures laid down by the company

- effectiveness of marketing thrust by the company

- list of issues difficult to resolve

- analysis of errors made and unsatisfactorily resolved

- features of management of conflict between business unit and project team

- list of personal qualities required of a top performer in the role of relationship management

- list of skills required in the same role

- outline of action that you would take to improve things if you were made CEO for a week.

By adopting this type of approach, the personal characteristics of the very best people can be determined, not only from purely a statistical point of view, but by insight into their personal working methods, desires, motivation, satisfaction levels and their potential capability.

From this, a profile can be built up to provide a yardstick by which top performers can be identified and, further, provide a guide to future hiring excellence.

CHAPTER 8

The Operational Role of HR

A HISTORICAL PERSPECTIVE

THE DEVELOPMENT OF PEOPLE MANAGEMENT

Many of the current activities of the HR function have been with us since the dawn of history. The earliest manifestations were the desires on the parts of emperors, kings and rulers to assemble groups of people in the form of armies in order to defend or extend their political power.

These organizations required lines of control in order to operate as cohesive units and so they became early examples of hierarchical structures. As military technology advanced, so specialist skills became necessary which in turn generated a requirement for training and the development of technical competence.

The observation by the Duke of Wellington that 'an army marches on its stomach' demonstrated the awareness that the employer had a variety of obligations to its members including 'pay and rations'. If these were not provided in an adequate or reliable manner, then morale and motivation would suffer.

Assembling bodies of men to engage in military activities introduced the early application of recruiting procedures together with the need to 'sell the concept' to the general populace in order to attract sufficient numbers of volunteers.

The hierarchical nature of military organizations was based upon the need to have clear leadership roles filled by people who understood how to implement strategic objectives. This requirement generated the 'officer class', a group of individuals who by virtue of training and experience (and for many centuries by birth or social class) could be entrusted with the role of leading their forces in hazardous activities.

These hazardous activities, frequently accompanied by poor food and uncomfortable living conditions, often caused desertions from the ranks or breaches of discipline. As a consequence there was a need to keep a record of the resources available to undertake their functions and to identify those who had broken the rules.

Absences from the ranks due to illness, injury, leave or desertion had to be accounted for if the managers (officers) were going to be able to perform their functions.

THE IMPACT OF THE INDUSTRIAL REVOLUTION

Similar considerations also applied when the growth of the Industrial Revolution required the assembly of large workforces in order to satisfy the manpower requirements of the new factories and manufacturing plants. Factory workers were largely recruited from the agricultural sector and so needed to be housed in close proximity to the workplace and trained in the processes to be employed. The use of machinery as the major contributor to mass production also introduced a new concept – health and safety. Scarce skills in various aspects of production were seen as valuable assets and so needed to be protected in the workplace and appropriate precautions introduced.

Throughout this historical period the various elements of the modern HR function were developed. They came about not because of any conscious effort to develop them but in response to specific needs and requirements.

The fundamental processes of recruitment, retention, training, payroll, record keeping, and health and safety, as well as communication and the development of organizational structures, were all developed in the face of specific operational requirements. As time has progressed, so the various techniques have been, and continue to be, refined.

POLITICS AND LEGISLATION

Much of the stimulation for improvements in working conditions came from social and legislative pressures. Enlightened employers quickly saw the commercial advantages of having a contented and capable workforce and, while their motivations may well have been based upon financial advantage, they were the inventors of the modern welfare state. The need to make provision for education, health care and retirement were all born out of the conditions created by the Industrial Revolution in the nineteenth century and the recognition of the value of national human assets.

Although they probably did not recognize it, the early and subsequent proponents of changes in employment conditions and the quality of the pool from which the workforce was drawn were another manifestation of the development of the modern HR function.

HR AND GLOBALIZATION

The development of the global corporation with customers, suppliers and delivery capabilities spread across a number of countries has added a new dimension to the HR function. One of the key drivers for this strategy is the desire to take advantage of cost differentials and international market potential.

From the HR perspective this requires the development of local capabilities which reflect local conditions while at the same time maintaining a common approach to employment policies and strategies.

In many global organizations there is a desire to identify high achievers in any location in order to develop an international talent pool which can be used to resource specific requirements as they emerge in any part of the global organization.

FROM PERSONNEL TO HR

THE DEVELOPMENT OF THE PERSONNEL DEPARTMENT

The forerunner to the HR function was the personnel department and before that there was the individual personnel manager.

In the middle of the twentieth century the personnel department started to take shape. The administrative functions such as payroll and record keeping largely resided in the departments of finance and accounts and for many years the personnel department, as it expanded, was a component of this function. In many organizations the head of personnel was an ex-military officer who was assumed to have expertise in people management and processes. Whether or not he (for it generally was a man who took the role) had any real understanding of the dimensions of this role was largely left to chance.

As the post-war economies began to expand there was a greater need to address recruitment and retention issues and so the department was expanded to include a recruitment function. Due to the rapid expansion of tertiary education and the greater availability of university graduates, the recruitment function added graduate recruitment to its operating scope.

The rapid spread of the use of computing technology in the 1960s and the resultant increase in business complexity generated a new dimension for the personnel department in the form of a requirement for training programmes, induction courses and educational materials.

Throughout this period the personnel function was largely operating in response mode. As each new challenge emerged, it responded by adding further resources and seeking a greater share of the operating budget.

THE BIRTH OF THE HR FUNCTION

At some stage the size and cost of the personnel function began to attract management attention and an interest developed in how its activities could be rationalized.

Computerization provided one solution. Payroll and record keeping could be automated or sub-contracted to one of the growing population of computer-based payroll services. Recruitment and selection agencies could be used to undertake much of the processing and administrative workload associated with hiring new staff. Search and selection firms could be used to help recruit additional senior staff and identify board appointees.

Education and training could also be outsourced either by buying places on public courses or through the employment of external training companies to deliver specific internal training programmes.

The underlying motivation was to move from fixed to variable costs in which a smaller core team would buy externally supplied services on an as-required basis, thereby reducing the size of the fixed-cost element.

This was really the trigger for the transition from personnel department to HR function. The HR function needed skills and resources which could determine needs and contract with external suppliers for their delivery.

They had to find a balance between what had to be done internally and what could be outsourced. The negotiation of these contracts required some forward planning and so the HR function started to take on a proactive role.

In most organizations headcount numbers are a key to power and influence. With the reduction in size of the personnel department and the introduction of a smaller but focused HR function, there was an implicit threat to the power and prestige of the head of that function.

STRATEGIC ROLE OF THE HR FUNCTION

The classic defence in such circumstances is to add value and to have the value valued. This introduced a new concept – HR business alignment.

HR executives started to investigate areas where their expertise and that of their colleagues in the HR function could demonstrate that they added value to the organization. An equivalent process was being undertaken by the IT function where, through outsourcing and increasing levels of IT literacy, the hitherto unchallenged need for increased corporate funding had been put under the microscope.

In both cases a similar strategy was adopted – business objectives alignment. This means that the function needed to show that it made a measurable contribution to the achievement of the goals and objectives of the organization. The delivery of these benefits had to be achieved at economic costs and this stimulated an interest in performance metrics.

Other elements of the corporate infrastructure had been subjected to the same scrutiny and there emerged a general concept of capital asset management. Under this concept all elements of the organization were expected to demonstrate a contribution to the capital value of the enterprise.

THE DEVELOPMENT OF HUMAN CAPITAL

These considerations became a significant part of the development of the capitalization and hence the share price of the organization. Such issues as brand value, intellectual property and tangible assets were included in financial analyst calculations and began to take on a value equivalent to revenue and margin growth and earnings per share.

For the HR function, human capital became the driving theme; the concept being that the employees were the true asset of the organization and should be treated as a capital asset. Adding to the asset base, developing its value and delivering added value through it became the functional imperatives and reflect the current objectives of the HR function.

The HR function has come a long way in the last 50 years. It has transitioned from a largely staff role to one which has strategic dimensions and is predicted to play an increasingly important role in the development of organizations which have a focus on the future and the continued exploitation of emerging technologies through the use of human capital.

PROCESSES FOR PERFORMANCE

PROCESS MANAGEMENT IN HR

The HR function is largely driven by defined processes. While most of these processes will be under constant review in order to ensure that they reflect current 'best practice', the underlying objective is to ensure that they are conducted in a consistent and transparent manner.

With the progressive expansion of the use of computerization in the HR field, much of the administrative work can be automated and outsourced and in many cases it is.

What is left is largely in the areas where subjective assessments are required: recruitment, appraisals, training needs and disciplinary matters.

The processes adopted in each of these areas need to reflect a consistency and predictability in their approach. They also need to be transparent to those who are affected by them.

In the area of talent management it will be particularly important to show that individual performance and potential are consistently assessed and effectively administered. An important element in the development of trust in the talent management strategy will be the manner in which these issues are managed.

In Chapter 7 we considered the use of information technology as a powerful tool in HR administration and its application in a talent management strategy.

The practical problems involved in administering the human resources in a large organization are considerable. The need to keep accurate records of employee movement, absence, reviews and performance as well as statutory requirements associated with pay, tax, benefits and expense reimbursements is a fundamental part of the administrative burden.

There is a future requirement which relates to the field of employee relations and the development of an appropriate employer culture.

In many organizations these issues are documented in the form of a staff handbook. This is a dynamic publication because it will need to reflect changing requirements as new issues arise which require a precise definition of the corporate standpoint. The spread of IT creates both problems and opportunities:

system security and data integrity create their own demands for explicit policies as does the need to prevent abuse of the technology infrastructure.

When a talent management strategy is implemented it is important to ensure that the necessary processes are implemented in order to support it.

The core of the processes will tend to relate to performance appraisal and potential assessment. The key to their success will be the clarity of their definition and the transparency of their application.

There are five key areas in which processes need to be defined and developed:

Goal setting and objectives

High achievers need specific goals and objectives against which to test their capabilities. Being assigned a role is not sufficient: there must be defined performance metrics combined with demonstration of management capabilities.

Performance assessment

The basis on which actual performance is assessed should be clearly defined. Some elements will be capable of precise measurement (the metrics), while others dealing with soft skills (mentoring, coaching, leadership and so on) will be subject to subjective scoring. Some care will be needed in determining how this scoring will be applied in order to be able to demonstrate consistency.

Knowledge assessment

As a result of training courses attended or the development of subject matter expertise through practical experience it would be anticipated that knowledge levels will increase. The measurement of knowledge levels in relevant areas should be a part of the overall performance assessment. In Chapter 4 we described the use and development of knowledge assessment techniques.

Skills assessment

These particularly relate to the development of skills in the management competency set. These will include:

- leadership
- coaching and mentoring
- decision-making

- communication

- planning.

The assessment will measure current levels of competency in relevant areas and may identify areas where specific improvement is required.

Potential assessment

'Past performance predicts future potential' is a common concept but it is important to allow for variations. One is the 'late developer' who suddenly brings everything together and emerges from the pack as a surprise star. The alternative is the rising star who stumbles and shows signs of peaking.

In determining future potential it will be necessary to take into account the results of the performance, knowledge and skills assessments, but also to make allowance for trends in performance which could indicate a need to review previous 'potential' rankings.

While performance reviews and capability assessments would generally be applied to all employees, they play a particularly important role in a talent management strategy because they are the formal ways of justifying the presence of an individual in a talent pool.

HR AND TALENT MANAGEMENT

INTRODUCTION

So far we have looked at how the modern HR function has developed and its role in contributing to the achievement of organizational objectives. We also saw the basis for the increasing focus in treating human resources as a capital asset.

In this section we look at the part that the HR function will play in the development and implementation of a talent management strategy.

SETTING THE SCENE

Talent management is a relatively new concept. As such it is unlikely that the majority of HR professionals will have a full understanding of the processes and practices involved in its implementation. The evidence for this assertion is the recruitment advertisements placed by large corporates for applicants for the roles of 'Director of Talent Management' or 'Head of Talent Management

Development'. Clearly there is a belief that this function requires specialist expertise which is beyond that of the typical HR professional.

Whether or not this is true, the impression exists that the development of a talent management strategy requires specialist expertise which is separate from the norm and is a scarce resource which commands differentiated rewards.

There is no doubt that the design, development and implementation of a corporate talent management strategy adds a new dimension to the HR function and requires an additional skill set.

DEVELOPING THE BUSINESS CASE

The development and implementation of a talent management strategy will require some investment. In return it is expected to deliver some benefits. The business case will be based upon the relationship between the predicted costs and the expected returns.

In a classic business-case scenario there will be an attempt to relate the costs to the returns, and calculate a return on investment (ROI) and a pay-back period (the length of time required for the cumulative value of the returns to equal the cost of the investment).

While it may not be possible to identify actual monetary values to some of the cost and benefit elements it is a useful exercise in which to identify what these elements are likely to be and the impact they are likely to have.

On the cost side the additional investment is likely to occur in the following areas:

- acquisition of specialist talent management expertise
- time and cost involved in developing the strategy
- time and cost involved in implementing the strategy
- time and cost involved in managing the strategy
- additional cost for specialist training programmes
- additional cost for selection and assessment processes.

It is assumed that the existing HR processes for conducting performance reviews and appraisals, managing appointments and providing training in internal processes and procedures will be adequate to support the talent management strategy.

On the benefit side the anticipated returns will include the following:

- reduction in staff turnover figures with a consequent reduction in recruitment costs

- the progressive development of a pool of high achievers, thus reducing the need to recruit expensive external skills

- an overall improvement in operational performance due to the impact of the high achieving pool of talent

- greater operational flexibility due to access to a pool of talent that can be deployed to manage new opportunities or challenging situations.

These benefits are in addition to those which are derived from the deliberate attempt to recruit, retain and develop a pool of high achievers with the consequent impact upon business performance and the image of the organization. The fact that so many organizations are adopting a talent management strategy as part of their desire to improve the use of their human capital shows that the business case for this approach is now fairly well established.

DEVELOPING THE STRATEGY

Once the decision has been taken to implement a talent management strategy, the HR function becomes deeply involved in its development and deployment.

As with any other project, it is important to make a distinction between planning and implementation. The planning stage will contain three elements:

- What do we want to achieve?

- What do we have now?

- What changes do we need to make?

The first element will involve the development of the strategic intent – what do we want to achieve? As the development and implementation of a talent management strategy is likely to be an executive decision it is probable that there will be some discussion about the objectives at board level. What is important is to have a clear definition of the objectives of the strategy because this will be necessary in order to construct a programme which will deliver the desired results.

At the executive level the objectives are likely to be expressed in terms which will directly affect the performance of the organization. As such they will probably identify the following objectives:

- raise the level of competence of management and junior executives

- provide for succession planning from internal resources

- develop a pool of high achievers which can be tapped to support growth plans.

The HR function is likely to have a slightly different agenda which includes the following:

- reduce staff turnover levels

- make it easier to attract high-calibre staff

- provide a basis for a structured training programme.

These different agendas are not mutually exclusive: they just reflect the different operational perspectives. The objective is to develop a definition of the strategic objectives which has universal acceptance as well as having practical and deliverable components.

Once the strategic objectives definition has been compiled and agreed, the next stage in the project is to plan how they will be achieved. The starting point is the current situation – what do we have now?

The existing HR functions and processes will need to be reviewed in order to determine what additions and changes will be required in order to deliver the desired outcomes expressed in the strategic objectives.

Specific areas for attention will include the following:

- selection and recruitment processes

- career development programmes

- coaching and mentoring provisions

- assessment and appraisal processes

- promotion selection procedures

- training and education programmes

- succession planning

- personal goal setting

- compensation and recognition programmes.

In each of these areas it will be necessary to identify where changes or additions will need to be made. The objective is to address the final part of the planning agenda – what changes do we need to make?

Once these changes have been identified, it is possible to begin the planning process for their implementation.

One important issue at this stage is how the strategy is positioned for external and internal consumption. The intention to develop and implement a talent management strategy will attract considerable internal attention, some of which will be suspicion and uncertainty about the underlying objectives. It will be important to position the intention as a positive step which has the objective of achieving overall operational excellence as well as providing avenues for career development and enhanced personal opportunities.

The description of the supporting processes, training programmes and mentoring arrangements will all help to develop internal support especially if it is coupled with senior executive sponsorship.

The development of the component of the talent management strategy will place a considerable additional load upon the HR function and may require the use of external specialists who have experience in this area. One interesting consideration is the qualities and competencies of a talented HR executive and the extent to which the employees of the existing HR function would satisfy these tests.

BUILDING THE PROGRAMME

The recommendation is to treat the implementation of the talent management strategy as a project. As such it will have tasks to complete, delivery schedules, resource requirements and a budget. It will also need a project leader who will be responsible for the delivery and implementation of the programme. It is most probable that the project leader will come from the HR function or may be a talent management specialist recruited for this purpose. Because of the nature of the project it will also require executive sponsorship so that it has visibility at executive levels.

As with any project the starting point is the identification of the constituent elements and the development of an overall project plan.

Each component needs to be examined under the following headings:

- Is this a new function or do we have it already?

- If it already exists, does it need to be changed?

- If it is a new function, can we develop it ourselves?

- Do we need external assistance to develop this function?

- What are the time and cost budgets of implementing this function?

Once each element has been deconstructed in this way, the next stage is to develop an outline implementation plan showing the sequence of implementation together with any elements which have a degree of interdependence and so need to be implemented in parallel.

For example, the selection and recruitment component could contain the following elements:

- psychometric testing

- knowledge assessment

- interview processes and techniques

- reference checking

- candidate process management

- medical checks

- job offer processing.

Clearly this component has a number of inter-related elements, all of which need to be defined and implemented in the form of a cohesive unit.

Not only does each component need to be developed, it also has to be documented so that the users can understand how to use it. This follows the standard project sequence of design, develop, document.

For new processes it will be necessary to introduce a further dimension – test. For the overall programme to achieve its objectives there must be universal acceptance and understanding of it. If some elements fail to pass this test, then the overall success level will be prejudiced.

Where new processes are to be introduced it is useful to expose them to a trial process with a selected test group so that any operational difficulties can be identified and remedied before the process is implemented.

The project plan will not only identify the components of the strategy and what will be involved in developing them but should also describe the implementation schedule and roll-out programme.

From experience it is preferable to implement a strategic programme of this type on a stage-by-stage basis over a period of time. This allows each component to 'bed in' and gain acceptance before the next element is introduced.

IMPLEMENTING THE STRATEGY

The recommended implementation strategy is the progressive implementation of each component on a staged basis.

For each component implementation it will be necessary to plan the following activities:

- internal communication on the purpose of the component and how it fits into the overall talent management strategy

- development of training programmes and supporting documentation to help users understand how to use the component

- implementation of the component and the provision of user support facilities

- establishment of a monitoring process designed to ensure that the implementation of the components is having the desired effect.

The staff handbook will also need to be updated with changes to existing processes and the addition of new ones. The existence of a talent management strategy should also be communicated in recruitment advertising and selection processes.

A further dimension to the implementation programme will be potential use of external suppliers to provide specialist services that will be used to support various components. These could be required in any of the following areas:

- psychometric testing as part of the selection process

- specialized training courses in such areas as leadership, communication and presentation skills, planning and performance appraisal

- assessment and review processes

- compensation and benefits planning.

The selection of suitable external suppliers and their integration into the overall strategy need to be included in the implementation programme.

SUPPORTING THE STRATEGY

Once the full strategy has been implemented, it will require constant attention from the HR function to ensure that the various components are being used as they should and that the strategy becomes embedded into the culture and fabric of the organization.

An important element of the strategy is the need to capture and record information about individual performance and progress. In Chapter 7 we discuss the use of IT and the structure of a database suitable as a storage and recording platform. As with any other computer application, the effectiveness of the system will depend upon the accuracy of the information contained within it. Quality control and data validation will consequently require some attention and this is likely to be an HR responsibility.

The capture of most of the information will be a result of the completion of various processes and so it will be equally important to ensure that these are correctly applied. This is a second aspect of quality control and in the early days it may be necessary for HR to take the role of observer or expert advisor to guide participants through the processes.

These two issues, data quality and process delivery, are operational considerations and as indicated are likely to require HR participation. A further consideration will be the need to demonstrate that the strategy is delivering the desired results and that the operational benefits are being obtained.

PROVING THE STRATEGY

Proving the talent management strategy requires the demonstration that the various components are in place, that they are being executed and that there are some manifestations that the desired outcomes are being delivered.

The three elements to be considered are:

- process

- practice

- performance.

It will be necessary to show that the relevant elements are in existence and that they are being correctly applied.

Process

This aspect requires validation that the relevant processes have been developed and that those who are required to execute them have been trained in their use, application and deployment.

Practice

This aspect requires confirmation that the processes are being correctly applied and that the outcomes demonstrate that the processes are delivering the desired results.

Performance

The performance dimension is the measure of the effectiveness of the overall strategy. By its very nature the talent management strategy will take some time to deliver all of its expected results, but it should be possible to demonstrate that it is moving in the right direction by showing that the processes and practices are having an impact in the following areas:

- recruitment and selection
- structured training programme
- appraisals and performance reviews
- knowledge assessments
- goal setting and performance targets.

It may be a useful exercise to conduct staff attitude surveys which are designed to measure the extent to which the strategy is recognized by the employees and their reactions to it.

From an HR perspective it will be important to demonstrate that the various elements of the strategy are in existence and that they are being executed in the desired manner. The executive concern will be about whether the strategy is capable of delivering the desired outcomes. Proving that the processes and practices are in place will be a valuable step towards building executive confidence in the overall programme.

SOME HUMAN CONSIDERATIONS

The HR function has traditionally held the role of the 'people guardian' in the organization.

Such issues as 'work and safety' and career counselling are manifestations of this role and demonstrate a professional responsibility for employee welfare.

The development and implementation of a talent management strategy raises a number of intellectual and even ethical challenges that may cause some concern for some HR professionals.

HIGH ACHIEVERS AS A SELECT GROUP

Throughout this book we have been considering the concept of identifying and developing individuals who have the potential to become superior performers and high achievers. We have described processes designed to recruit, develop and retain these individuals, plus the need for coaches and mentors who will assist in their skills and career development.

Membership of this group will be a mark of recognition and an aspirational goal for the majority of the employees. But how do people feel who are not in this select group?

There is some evidence that the very existence of a talent elite acts as a demotivator to other employees, especially if it is believed that those outside the group are regarded as inferior and are given fewer opportunities for career development.

Clearly such a perception must be countered, but not at the expense of diluting the focus on developing a solid core of high achievers.

There is a view that any talent management strategy should be company-wide and inclusive: all employees should have an equal opportunity to develop their potential. However, such an approach flies in the face of logic. Not everyone has the skills and intellect to become a brain surgeon or rocket scientist but those that do not are not lesser beings. What is important is to have a career development strategy which encourages every individual to develop their full potential while at the same time recognizing that there will be some who, through aptitude, intellect and application, are capable of handling rapid advancement and wider responsibilities.

The members of this group are valuable assets and any inclusive talent management strategy must have the capacity to identify them and provide separate or specialized career development support.

Finding the right balance between an identified and possibly divisive elite and a generic inclusive approach to talent management will depend upon the culture of the organization and the strategic imperative that is adopted; however, both alternatives deserve consideration and the HR function has a responsibility to identify them.

WORK/LIFE BALANCE

There is a general belief that one of the characteristics of high achievers is stamina. Their primary focus is upon work and they are prepared and able to devote most of their waking hours to it. This is often at the expense of their personal relationships, outside interests and even their health. Those who fall from this high standard are sidelined or moved to lower profile roles.

In the age when there was an implicit contract between the employer and the employee relating to lifetime employment, those who were prepared to make personal sacrifices could justify them on the basis that there would be personal rewards.

Current business practices have shown that the expectation of lifetime employment is no longer a viable consideration. The impact of downsizing, outsourcing and offshore operations have all demonstrated that employers are liable to take actions that challenge these assumptions. As a result, employees are taking a more pragmatic approach to their relationships with their employers and are prepared to change jobs if they see impending threats to their future careers.

A key element in any talent management strategy is the need to retain high achievers, therefore practices need to be developed that reflect current employment conditions. Able people are more likely to move between employers because of their inherent qualities. They are also high-profile targets for headhunters and so are made aware of their potential value to other employers.

If the concept of lifetime employment is one casualty of the changes in the business environment, so also are the expectations of work commitment.

The development of the global market coupled with the availability of 24/7 communications has created both challenges and opportunities.

The challenges are the pressures on time imposed by immediate and continuous access by and to the individual. The tyranny of the Internet coupled with mobile personal communications means that the individual is always 'on'. The effective management of the demands of instant communication is becoming one of the key requirements of the high achiever.

The opportunities that instant and mobile communications present also allow for different forms of work style, of which homeworking is probably the most common. The ability to access corporate information from a remote location, plus the ability to communicate directly with colleagues, customers and suppliers via the Internet or mobile phone, means that the home office is a viable alternative to a permanent office location.

The mobile worker is able to adopt a more flexible work style and thus is able to pursue a more balanced use of time and resources and find a more acceptable work/life balance.

Employers are starting to realize the need to provide their employees with the means of achieving a better work/life balance, partly because of the economic benefits and partly due to social demands.

From the perspective of retaining high achievers, one increasingly important consideration will be the extent to which facilities are provided which enable these employees to deploy their expertise in a way which supports an acceptable work/life balance.

If the concept of lifetime employment has largely disappeared, so also has the concept of absolute devotion to work at the expense of lifestyle considerations.

SUMMARY

The HR function is the key driver of the talent management strategy. It will be involved in every aspect of its design, deployment and effective operation. In each of these aspects it will have to take account of internal and external cultural forces and ensure that the strategy delivers the required results within the context of these issues.

CASE STUDIES

CASE STUDY 1: TALENT MANAGEMENT STRATEGY – HOW TO GET IT WRONG

The following is a dialogue and summary of an attempt to develop a talent management strategy which went badly wrong. Readers may identify with some of the sentiments expressed and the behavioural patterns. This case study is based on a number of experiences and so presents a composite picture.

> Email
> From: Managing Director
> To: HR Director
> Subject: Talent management
>
> *On my recent business trip I read an article in a management magazine extolling the virtues of a talent management strategy. Looks good to me, I have attached a copy.*
>
> *Let me have your thoughts on whether it is right for us in time for the board meeting on Thursday.*

✳ ✳ ✳

> Email
> From: HR Director
> To: Managing Director
> Subject: Talent management
>
> *As you know we are in the middle of the annual wages round for which you want a report by Thursday; as a result, I have only been able to give the article a general review. This approach appears to be aimed at management levels and so has little relevance to the bulk of our employees who are factory workers. It would take time and cost to implement and may be a bit adventurous for us. Management turnover is high enough without provoking possible resentment. Hope this helps.*

✳ ✳ ✳

> Email
> From: Managing Director
> To: HR Director
> Subject: Talent management strategy
>
> *In spite of your hopes, your reply on the above subject was not helpful. I had also circulated the article to our non-executives who all thought it a*

practical step and that we should be more 'adventurous'. The board has decided to implement a talent management strategy and I have assured them of your positive and active support.

Let me have an outline plan within the next two weeks.

I was disappointed with your recommendations on the wages round; fix a meeting with me and the Finance Director to discuss.

✳ ✳ ✳

Email
From: HR Director
To: Managing Director
Cc: Finance Director
Subject: Talent management strategy

In an attempt to put together an outline plan as requested I have done some research on the Internet into the subject. It appears to be a bigger step than the article you read suggests. This is a specialist field and we will need to recruit a senior person to run the programme. There will also be additional costs associated with training, coaching and skills development. My current budget will not cover these expenses. The outline plan will describe a programme which we can implement over the next two years together with an operating budget.

✳ ✳ ✳

Email
From: Managing Director
To: HR Director
Cc: Finance Director
Subject: Talent management strategy

Why is it that every time I ask for some action from HR all I get in response is a request for more staff and a bigger budget? I cannot understand why you can't release one of your many staff to resolve this issue; if I ran the company in the way you run your department we would go to the wall. I look forward to reading your report but do not expect to see any additional costs associated with it – if necessary cut back on some of your other activities.

✳ ✳ ✳

Email

From: HR Director
To: Managing Director
Subject: Talent management strategy
Attachment: Outline project plan

Please find attached the outline project plan for developing and implementing a talent management strategy as requested. The costs of implementing this programme are identified and will be covered by making cuts in existing programmes, including health and safety training, induction courses, internal communications and updating the staff handbook. The leader of the project will be Susie Smith who has attended a seminar on talent management.

✳ ✳ ✳

Email

From: Managing Director
To: HR Director
Subject: Talent management project plan

I have circulated your plan to the board and the executive directors, they are in general agreement but are surprised at the time you think it will take to develop and implement the project. Please let me have a revised timetable which demonstrates your understanding of the urgency of the need to get some results in the near future.

✳ ✳ ✳

Email

From: HR Director
To: Managing Director
Subject: Talent management project plan
Attachment: Revised development and implementation
               schedule

Please find attached the revised development and implementation schedule as requested. If I could allocate more resources to the development phase we could shorten the schedule; as it is, the revised deadlines are tight and we will not have time to test some of the elements of the programme prior to implementation. The schedule will also be affected because Susie Smith has just applied for maternity leave.

✳ ✳ ✳

Email

From: Managing Director
To: HR Director
Subject: Revised development plan for talent
                 management

Your new schedule is accepted. Please commence the project immediately and keep me posted on progress. Let me know how you plan to cover for the absence of Mrs Smith and how you will ensure that there is no project slippage.

The board would like to have your assessment of the benefits of this programme in financial terms together with a risk assessment and an indication of the return on investment.

❋ ❋ ❋

Email

From: HR Director
To: Managing Director
Subject: Revised plan and investment report

Mrs Smith says she can do some work from home but I have had to take on a contractor to fill her slot in Staff Relations anyway. I will attempt to fill some of the gap myself and will be attending a short course on talent management in two weeks' time. I am sending you separately my assessment of the areas where the programme will deliver financial benefits but some aspects can only be subjective. I would expect most of the benefits to be in the area of reduced management-level staff turnover but will have a better feel after attending the course.

❋ ❋ ❋

Email

From: Managing Director
To: HR Director
Subject: Talent management strategy

I am glad that you are finally taking this project seriously and getting involved yourself. You are no doubt aware that while you are away on your course we shall be reviewing the first pass of the operating budget for next year. I am sure that we will have your detailed submissions available in time for the review. Please let me have an assessment of the contents of the course on your return and whether you think the cost was justified.

SUMMARY

It will be obvious to the reader from the above series of communications that this project has all the ingredients of a serious failure. However, the characteristics are not uncommon and justify some analysis.

- *Call for action.* It is not uncommon for managing directors to pick up a theme that they think will be beneficial to the company; logical argument is the only way to manage expectations.

- *Response to the request.* The HR Director went on the defensive which compromised his negotiating position; a better response would have been to show enthusiasm but tempered with the need to gather the facts on the implications before identifying problems.

- *Building the case.* It would have been better to develop a working party with the executives and the board which would have the objectives of exploring the potential benefits of the strategy so that they could be related to potential costs. This would have strengthened the hand of the HR Director in terms of getting appropriate financial backing.

- *Developing the budget.* Once the HR Director had acceptance of the potential benefits and agreement that most were subjective, the construction of the project budget should have been based on the costs of doing the job well; trying to do it on the cheap would have compromised the benefits to be obtained.

- *Recognizing that special skills were needed.* Again, by building a team approach with the executives it would be possible to explore why it was necessary to recruit specialist skills to lead the development and implementation of the programme; it would also have been useful to seek information from other companies that had implemented a talent management strategy to obtain advice on how to make a success of the project.

- *Operating under pressure.* Allowing for poetic licence in the above narrative, one of the important points is that any new strategy has to be implemented within the context of existing needs and pressures. This means that the time, resource and cost budgets for implementing a talent management strategy have to be treated as an additional activity.

CHAPTER 9

Assess Your Own Knowledge of Talent Management Using a Talent Management Corporate Profile

IS YOUR ORGANIZATION READY TO IMPLEMENT A TALENT MANAGEMENT PROGRAMME?

Having read Chapters 1–8, you may be thinking that the implementation of a talent management programme would be of considerable value to your company.

You may be a senior executive involved in various operations charged with developing many functions within the organization or a specialist department responsible for a programme of major improvement in, say, business analysis or project management.

The following questionnaire will help you and your company to determine whether you are currently able to implement a talent management programme, or what new procedures you might need to put into place in order to effect the best processes and changes. As in many multi-choice questionnaires, there are best answers, good answers and both neutral and wrong answers. This profile is designed to help you highlight the best or preferred answers and disregard those that are only possibly correct. After all, this is a questionnaire on talent management where only the best will do!

TALENT MANAGEMENT CORPORATE PROFILE

Q.1: What is talent management?

You may select only one answer.

    a)   A special aptitude or faculty

    b)   Exceptional mental ability in problem-solving

c)   Hiring, developing and retaining the best people.

Q.2: Many companies believe in promoting only from within for senior appointments. What's your view?

You may select only one answer.

a)   Desirable

b)   Undesirable

c)   Doesn't matter.

Q.3: It's best initially to identify talent internally rather than go out to the market. What do you think?

You may select only one answer.

a)   Internal – because of their knowledge of the organization

b)   External – because new blood is always preferable

c)   Doesn't matter.

Q.4: Which of the following is *not* one of the elements in a Talent Search Matrix?

You may select only one answer.

a)   Experience

b)   Expertise

c)   Profile

d)   Potential

e)   Qualification

f)   Quality.

Q.5: Which of the following are necessary in order to deliver superior results?

You may select more than one answer.

a)   Assess the nature of the challenge

b)   Understand the motivation of the supporting team

c)   Identify the key performance metrics

d)   Determine how to achieve them

e)   Implement the plan

f)   Monitor the results.

Q.6: Change can be seen as a disruption or a welcome contribution to corporate development. How would a talented person view change, even if the apparent change process were not necessarily an immediate positive contribution to organization development but could have future benefit?

You may select only one answer.

a)   Essential

b)   Unnecessary

c)   Desirable.

Q.7: Are talented people inherently curious and do they seek further knowledge in a formal environment or do they develop by experience?

You may select more than one answer.

a)   They just pick things up naturally

b)   They welcome formal training events

c)   They self-study regularly

d)   They elect to do higher degree courses, for example MBA, PhD if appropriate.

Q.8: At board level, the following questions re talent management might be asked. Which of the following are relevant in your own organization?

You may select more than one answer.

a)   We want to recruit, retain and develop talented people in our company.

b)   We know who the really talented people are in our company.

c)   We have a programme in place regarding succession planning.

d)   We know what management skills and resources we need for the foreseeable future.

e)   We can now implement a talent management programme.

Q.9: In terms of defining the knowledge required in order to develop the necessary talent, which of the following are needed in order to develop the factors involved in measuring the knowledge profile?

You may select more than one answer.

a)   Define the body of knowledge involved for the assessment in question

b)   Assess the current levels

c)   Identify where the knowledge gaps lie

d)   Deliver training and coaching to fill the gaps.

Q.10: Talent management inevitably involves change management. There are a number of stages included in a change process. Which of the following are key to managing change?

You may select up to four answers.

a)   How the need for the change arose

b)   Analysis of the situation

c)   Determination of the changes required

d)   Execution of the changes

e)   Involvement of everyone likely to be affected by the changes

f)   Effect of the changes

g)   Reinforcement of the change programme.

Q.11: Talented people will adapt to change more readily providing that certain steps are taken. Which of the following will assist in this process?

You may select up to four answers.

a)   The reason for the change is explained.

b)   Training is provided in the new processes.

c)   Everyone is given the opportunity to question the changes at any time prior to the implementation of such changes.

d)   Support is provided in the change period.

e)   Senior management keeps the impact of the change confidential.

    f)   Everyone involved in the change process is advised of the outcome.

Q.12: If a company has a people-supporting culture, which of the following characteristics would you expect to be in place?

You may select more than one answer.

    a)   A structured recruitment process

    b)   A formal development and training programme

    c)   A formal promotion board

    d)   An annual counselling and appraisal system

    e)   A strong HR function

    f)   An Open Door policy

    g)   Clear policies for preserving the dignity of the individual.

Q.13: Most companies use some form of testing or assessment for new hires, promotables and so on. In the case of psychometric testing, which of the following are covered by such tests?

You may select up to three answers.

    a)   Attitude

    b)   Knowledge

    c)   Aptitude

    d)   Technical capability

    e)   Personality.

Q.14: In hiring a senior manager, which of the following attributes would you expect to measure using psychometric assessment methods?

You may select more than one answer.

    a)   Intellectual capacity (IQ)

    b)   Emotional maturity (EQ)

    c)   Communication ability

    d)   Necessary job skills

e)   Evidence of commitment

f)   Self-awareness

g)   Determination and energy.

Q.15: Which of the following are generally claimed as being the proven benefits of psychometric testing in a talent management environment?

You may select more than one answer.

a)   Objective measurement

b)   Consistency

c)   Predictors of performance

d)   Close assessment of candidate's self-awareness

e)   Insight into team performance

f)   Cost effectiveness.

Q.16: Knowledge assessment (KA) is different from psychometric testing for a number of reasons. However, some people tend to confuse the two methods. Which of the following are the prerequisites for a knowledge assessment process?

You may select more than one answer.

a)   KA requires a body of knowledge representing the subject matter.

b)   KA allows for multiple answers to many questions.

c)   KA needs to be validated by recognized specialist practitioners in the subject matter.

d)   KA only represents one-third of a total assessment spectrum.

e)   Behavioural characteristics are an additional part of a KA evaluation.

f)   A hiring decision can be made upon the result of a KA evaluation alone.

Q.17: The following are the key functions of knowledge assessment.

You may select more than one answer.

a)   Training needs analysis (TNA)

b)   Assessment of work rate

c)   Selection and recruitment

d)   Determination of commitment to the job

e)   Measuring effectiveness of training

f)   Managing talent

g)   Identification of promotables

h)   To see whether the candidate will match the job requirements

i)   Downsizing

j)   Acquisitions – to assess the quality of the inherited workforce.

Q.18: Talented people are said to have a collection of special characteristics.

Would you agree or disagree with the following characteristics of talented people?

a)   Identifying value and ensuring its delivery

[ ] Agree [ ] Disagree

b)   Reliable decision-making

[ ] Agree [ ] Disagree

c)   Consistency in management behaviour

[ ] Agree [ ] Disagree

d)   Managing and reinforcing change programmes

[ ] Agree [ ] Disagree

e)   Constantly questioning and seeking better solutions to established processes

[ ] Agree [ ] Disagree

f)   Practitioners of conflict management

[ ] Agree [ ] Disagree

Q.19: Irrespective of background, education and discipline, someone on a talent management programme needs more than just a superficial overview of finance.

Suggested topics might include, amongst others:

a)   Value theory and Earned Value Analysis

[ ] Agree [ ] Disagree

b)   Cost of capital

[ ] Agree [ ] Disagree

c)   DCF (Discounted Cash Flow)

[ ] Agree [ ] Disagree

d)   Risk management in financial terms

[ ] Agree [ ] Disagree

e)   Project evaluation and viability

[ ] Agree [ ] Disagree

f)   Project finance

[ ] Agree [ ] Disagree

g)   NPV (Net Present Value)

[ ] Agree [ ] Disagree

Q.20: Training for talented people might well be prescribed on the basis of a clear TNA derived from a knowledge assessment profile taken at a planned timescale according to a personal development programme. What, in your opinion, is the preferred method of assessing the effectiveness of the training?

You may select only one answer.

a)   Tell the trainee to present the key features of the training event

b)   Interview the trainee to determine the level of achievement

c)   Tell the trainee to re-sit a relevant knowledge assessment module.

Q.21: Does the presentation of change involve a simple statement of facts or does it require a detailed analysis of contributory factors designed to influence decision-makers so that they have a complete picture, thus enabling them to reach the correct decision?

Examine the following factors and select those that you feel are necessary in a structured change process. You may select more than one answer.

a)   Tell your audience that the change is essential and that there is no alternative

b)   Advise them what is currently wrong

c)   Present a possible solution

d)   Advise them how the solution will work

e)   Tell them what costs are involved

f)   Outline the benefits and timescale of achievement

g)   Tell them the consequences of not taking action.

Q.22: In presenting to your own senior management as part of a talent management review, which of the following factors need to be considered very carefully?

You may select more than one answer.

a)   The objective is purely to impart information.

b)   There is no need to have any other specific objectives.

c)   The content is more important than the strength of the presentation.

d)   Back-up visuals are not required as it is only an internal review.

e)   Your credibility is unlikely to be affected by a luke-warm performance.

Q.23: What are the main drawbacks present in many appraisal systems?

You may select more than one answer.

a)   Managers are not motivated to put in the effort.

b)   In order to make the interview as non-confrontational as possible, managers might rate a subordinate higher than is realistic.

c)   Some managers might be reluctant to rate a subordinate too highly for fear of losing a valuable resource.

d)   Some managers might downgrade a subordinate for 'spite'.

e)   The superior manager must sign off the documentation for the process.

f)   The employee needs to provide input in order for the process to be reliable.

Q.24: 360-degree assessment is better than one-to-one appraisal because it involves so many different interfaces.

[ ] True [ ] False

Q.25: In designing a talent management database, it is important to keep detailed records of the various monitoring controls to ensure the best quality management information. Which of the following are essential?

You may select more than one answer.

a) Details of personnel assigned to the programme

b) Knowledge assessment results

c) Academic and professional qualifications

d) Psychometric test results

e) Details of the career managers assigned to the programme

f) Course results.

Q.26: Talent management reports should have numerical measurement levels in additional to qualitative descriptions in order to facilitate comparisons for the appreciation of senior management.

[ ] Desirable [ ] Unnecessary

Q.27: The database system should have the facility to modify threshold 'norms' realistically to reflect the priority of subjects contained in the talent management programme.

[ ] Necessary [ ] Unnecessary

Q.28: In the transition from the traditional personnel department to a true HR function, which of the following significant changes took place?

You may select more than one answer.

a) Computerization

b) Use of recruitment agencies

c) Outsourcing of training services

d) Reduction of fixed costs

e) Smaller personnel presence.

Q.29: HR and IT might be described as evolving in a similar manner with regard to organization development. With which of the following do you agree?

You may select only one answer.

a)   HR and IT add value to an organization.

b)   Business objectives alignment is only relevant to IT.

c)   Employees need not be regarded as being a capital asset of the company.

Q.30: Processes relating to performance appraisal and assessment should be regarded as fundamental to the need to define some of the elements of a talent management strategy. Which of the following do you recognize as being essential?

You may select more than one answer.

a)   Objective setting

b)   Performance assessment

c)   Knowledge assessment

d)   Post-graduate qualifications

e)   Higher management potential

f)   Professional qualifications.

Q.31: Hiring people who have similar characteristics to your best employees may be a sound strategy. How do you measure the salient criteria to make a reasoned and justifiable decision whether or not to hire?

You may select more than one answer.

a)   Sustained excellence over at least a two-year period

b)   Positive behavioural characteristics

c)   Personal motivation and motivation of subordinates

d)   Knowledge of the requirements to do the job, now and in the future

e)   Impeccable pedigree with regards to experience

f)   Impressive presence and personality

g)   Distinguished personal background.

You have completed the questionnaire so now turn to Appendix B to see how your perception of talent management matches our answers.

CHAPTER 10

Summary

As we have seen, many companies are viewing talent management programmes as part of a significant contribution to future prosperity. But we also know that talented people will only stay with their current employer if opportunity is based upon positive development, motivation and nurturing to ensure that they are given every chance of realizing their potential.

Without the correct balance of these issues, experience has shown that the best people just leave and seek a better environment in which to develop and achieve their personal goals.

Simple financial packages, although superficially very attractive, often assuage a short-term need but rarely cater for the long-term requirements of a highly talented person who envisages a career leading to appointments at the most senior levels in both public and private sectors. The conclusion that can therefore be reached is that the offer of a 'golden' reward will only defer the inevitable. In the absence of serious support for the best people, separation often becomes the unfortunate, but inevitable result.

Another issue that has been found is that there is always the possibility that talented people will not always be required to call upon their exclusive talents to perform at the best possible levels. Line and staff managers must remain extremely sensitive to the effect of talent and every endeavour should be made to ensure that talent emerges and is used for optimum effect.

In this work, we have covered issues relating to selection and recruitment using various assessment methods, followed by performance measurement and prescribed training. But the key question we need to ask ourselves is: 'Having satisfied the initial established standards and criteria laid down by the company, is there a clear path to realizing the talent at subsequent levels of responsibility?' In other words, will the performance criteria that we expected be matched by actual results?

One lesson that has already been learned is that once the basics are identified, the key to reinforcement of expectation is the level at which ongoing management monitoring and development is maintained and enhanced. The issue that should never be overlooked is the alignment of prevailing capability of the individuals involved with the ever-changing short- and longer-terms needs of the business.

All too often, people needs and company needs are not managed in parallel. As we have covered earlier in this book, the ASK relationship needs to be at the forefront of any talent management operation. If any of the elements, attitude, skill or knowledge, are absent, a serious risk can be developed in terms of having the wrong person in what appeared to be the right job. A further definition that might be added is the 'experience' quotient. The reason why 'experience' is in quote marks is that, frequently, people who claim to have had 'ten years' experience' deliver a disappointing subsequent performance for their new management. The main reason for this is that some apparently talented people, or at least some of those who claim to be, have not had 'ten years' experience' but one year's experience ten times!

Let us return to the question of motivation of high-fliers.

Many people in business have acknowledged that there are four fundamental factors surrounding personal motivation. Of course, all of these can apply to any one person in many walks of life, but how can we apply it to highly talented people who are absolutely determined to achieve their challenging personal goals?

First of all, we need to look at the basic factors:

1.   money

2.   recognition

3.   opportunity

4.   job satisfaction.

What is the correct sequence for a person on a talent management programme? Is such a person primarily interested and motivated by money? Is job satisfaction more important? Are such people merely seeking opportunity? Or is recognition the key motivator?

Experience has shown that salespeople are primarily motivated by money but their motivation sequence based upon the above factors might be 1, 4, 3, 2.

Someone aspiring to a line management assignment might have the profile 3, 2, 1, 4.

A newly-appointed manager might feel that the optimum balance is 4, 1, 2, 3.

These profiles will vary from time to time depending upon prevailing desires, aspirations and circumstances.

But, coming back to people who have been identified as being high-fliers and enrolled on a talent management programme, their motivation may well be significantly different from that of only satisfactory performers.

What would their profile be on this basis?

Various surveys by different assignment types illustrated the following:

1. recognition

2. opportunity

3. job satisfaction

4. money.

Or, to put it another way, the sequence is 2, 3, 4, 1 based upon the original formula.

Moreover, the degree of variance dependent upon desires and aspirations was minimal. In other words, talented people were not necessarily satisfied with just the latest promotion; they sought the next move immediately upon their new appointment! They also realized that if they achieved their recognition, the other factors would all fall into place, particularly money, which becomes less important on its own and is commensurate with the achievement of the other factors.

Not all people see things this way.

Now, does this give us something of an insight into the differences in motivation between competent practitioners and those destined for the top? The most interesting factor is that recognition was invariably number 1. Why is this? One theory (or practice) is that if recognition is at the optimum level, it is more than likely that job satisfaction, money and opportunity are being taken care of very well and are not critical considerations for talented people.

So, perhaps as the main motivator, recognition might be seen as being the driver in identifying talent in key people and maybe we ought to consider this factor very carefully when assessing people as potential high-fliers.

As we have seen at various stages of this work, performance assessment or measurement helps us to identify all aspects of business effectiveness in the assigned role and as a pre-cursor for future responsibility. At the very least a talent management programme can set realistic and achievable performance levels and align commensurate compensation or reward mechanisms to encourage the achievement of set objectives. It can also do this over prescribed timescales to reduce the possibility of some people benefiting from pure luck.

Having mentioned luck, however, it is always interesting to hear that really talented people tend to generate their own luck.

A senior manager in an international distribution company was asked by his divisional director, 'Why is Joanna regularly failing to meet her objectives?' The answer was that Joanna had been 'unlucky'. The director responded, 'Surround yourself by lucky people!'

The fact is that really good people generate their own luck by concentrating all their efforts in the pursuit of their quest for excellence. After all, was it not Gary Player, the top-class golfer, who said, 'The more I practise, the luckier I get?'

It must be re-iterated that the focus of attention for successful talent management must reflect the needs of the individual within the objectives of the organization.

Perhaps the most welcome reaction from those people who are being nurtured by their company is that they feel 'completely understood'. Once that very satisfactory status is reached, we are well on the way to achieving one of the key objectives, retention.

It is thought that key people will stay if the environment within their organization is conducive to self-fulfilment, work is a fun place to be and people know that they are valued and can go 'the extra mile' with the knowledge that they will have the complete support of their management.

Unfortunately, this is not always the case. Recent data shows that slightly more than half of talented people have moved to alternative employers within the last three years. Therefore, the time has now come where this subject must be taken very seriously. Heavy investment in talented people must not be frittered away by lack of reinforcement. But it must be remembered that people will only stay if they want to.

In some multinational organizations, people, when asked, will say that 'this is not just a job – it's a way of life. I couldn't imagine not working for the company'. However, some of these people may not be those that the company really wishes to retain in its employment programme.

An interesting development, and perhaps one which few people might have anticipated, is that the pressure to attract more talent is greater than ever and very unlikely to reduce in intensity, irrespective of external economic conditions.

Therefore we are back to the basic premises of talent management.

We need to attract the right people, make them feel special, train them, give them every opportunity to develop, motivate them with realistic goals and rewards but, above all, keep them in the business.

Finally, is there a formula that guarantees success for talent retention?

In essence, probably not, but there are certain precautions we can take:

- Don't confuse retention in the long term with a one-off 'pay boost'.

- Ensure that the workplace is a great place to be.

- Encourage the fact that people's personal esteem is maintained at the highest possible level and be very aware that should the level diminish, this could result in discontent, one of the factors marking the beginning of separation.

- Constantly publicize personal development programmes to show that people's needs are seriously being addressed in the company in the case of both individuals and team platforms.

- Develop or purchase the best IT system to cover all aspects of information management.

- Work very closely with HR to ensure that everybody likely to be affected by the programme is regularly informed of its current status.

What we hope to have covered in this book is the fact that talent management should be reviewed and implemented in its ever-changing form at every stage of the company's development, from hiring, through development and promotion of the very best people. If talent adds value and quality to the business, do not underestimate or fail to realize its potential. But do not imagine that a talent management programme is self-supportive; it needs to be managed and adjusted to a wide range of functions and disciplines in order to provide the desired results and the return on its investment.

Most importantly, the very top of the organization must be seen to be totally committed to its success and this message – the pursuit, maintenance and continuing development of excellence – must permeate throughout the whole of the company.

In this way, prosperity in the future can be better assured.

CHAPTER 11

Guidelines for Creating a Talent Management System Based Upon Best Practices

THE PURSUIT OF EXCELLENCE

Having completed this work, we now need to consider how a talent management programme can be implemented in the most effective manner for those who have not considered such an approach before. The guidelines below spell out one approach but it is by no means the only way in which such a programme could be set up.

The following notes are provided to set up possible project parameters that will enable the new user to identify the best procedure for their company.

One of the objectives of the talent management strategy is to assemble and develop a pool of high achievers. While their inherent qualities will make them a valuable asset, it is their potential to make a significant contribution to the organization that sets them apart.

Exploiting this potential should be a strategic objective. People who do things well are generally in the best position to make suggestions on how to do them better. Tapping into this potential is how the exploitation is achieved.

DEVELOPMENT GROUPS

One observed practice is to establish a number of development groups. These are small teams of high achievers who are tasked with reviewing existing practices and processes with a view to identifying how and where performance improvements can be achieved.

The terms of reference of the development groups need to be precisely defined and the scope of operations kept quite narrow. This is because the members of the development groups have their normal responsibilities to handle and so what is sought is a short, sharp exercise aimed at delivering specific outcomes.

It is also important to ensure that the terms of reference contain performance metrics. The key objective is the delivery of measurable benefits.

Membership of the development groups will provide the high achievers with an opportunity to demonstrate their abilities to analyse problems, devise and specify practical solutions and identify quantifiable benefits. This in itself is a valuable training exercise and a preparation for future roles in which they will be responsible for the performance of various parts of the organization.

From experience it is useful to appoint a senior executive to act as a mentor to each development group. This will help to ensure that the development group does not explore options or solutions which will not fit into the current organization infrastructure or which will be in conflict with strategic directions. It also has the benefit of allowing the mentor to observe the behaviour and performance of individual members of the development group.

PERFORMANCE METRICS AND GOAL SETTING

In order for the development groups to focus their attention on developing solutions, which will deliver quantifiable benefits, it is important to include measurable reference points in the terms of reference. Inevitably the majority of the reference points will relate to costs and cost savings but some may be related to productivity levels or quality measures.

The following are examples of unstructured and structured terms of reference for a development group. Both are seeking essentially the same outcome but the structured version is much more likely to deliver a valuable contribution.

UNSTRUCTURED TERMS OF REFERENCE

> *'We are concerned about the time, cost and effort involved in our graduate recruitment programme. Please review the current processes and suggest ways in which they can be improved.'*

STRUCTURED TERMS OF REFERENCE

> *'We are concerned about the time, cost and effort involved in our graduate recruitment programme. Please identify the total costs involved in recruiting each graduate and identify ways in which they can be reduced without compromising the quality of the selection processes.'*

Clearly the second description is more likely to result in a report which will deliver quantifiable benefits and also provides the development group with a defined focal point.

The point about including performance metrics is that they require the development of 'before' and 'after' scenarios so that a quantifiable difference can be identified. They also stress the importance of gathering information before making a decision so that planned actions are based upon facts rather than impressions.

DEVELOPMENT GROUPS AS TRAINING PLATFORMS

In the example cited above, the development group will need to complete a number of tasks in order to arrive at a position where they can recommend an appropriate action.

These tasks would include:

- analyse the current graduate recruitment process

- identify all of the direct and indirect cost elements

- calculate the total cost incurred for each graduate recruit

- devise a process which can reduce the overall cost

- identify the costs of introducing the new process

- calculate the cost per recruit under the new process

- show the source and dimensions of the potential cost savings.

In completing these tasks the development group members will need to demonstrate their capabilities in the following areas:

- investigation and analysis

- cost attribution and quantification

- solution design and specification

- solution development and costing

- ROI and payback analysis.

These are all valuable skills to develop and apply to a real situation; the project will also allow the development group members to test their individual and collective capabilities. The real value of development groups is that they provide a basis for tapping into the capabilities of high achievers at a relatively early stage in their career while delivering quantifiable benefits to the organization.

Modular Sales Training Programme Course Appraisal

Course Modules: _____

Date: _____

Your evaluation of the Course as outlined below, is welcomed, with any further comments you would like to make.

Please rate the following 1 – 5, where 1 = poor, 5 = excellent by circling the number.

1)	Quality of preparation course material	1	2	3	4	5
2)	Quality of instruction	1	2	3	4	5
3)	Relevance to your own job now	1	2	3	4	5
4)	Relevance to known future assignments	1	2	3	4	5
5)	Ability of the Instructor to maintain interest	1	2	3	4	5
6)	Ability of the Instructor to handle questions	1	2	3	4	5
7)	Level of interaction by the Group	1	2	3	4	5
8)	The achievement of established course subjects	1	2	3	4	5
9)	Your level of motivation as a result of the course	1	2	3	4	5

Comments: Please indicate areas where you feel the course might be improved or any other areas for future training that would be of interest to you.

_____

_____

_____

_____

_____

_____

_____

_____

NAME	CLASS MANAGER			CALL/PRESENTATION	NO. COURSE

	G	S	W	

PREPARATION				
Organised/Prep				
Strategy				
Objectives				
Reference Sells				
Visuals				

TECHNIQUE				
Opening				
Questioning				
Establishing Need & Priority				
Listening				
Creating Interest				
Selling & Relating Benefits				
Handling Objections				
Checking for Agreement				
Summary & Close				
Using Visual Aids				
Flexibility & Control				
Action Plan				
Summary & Close				

PERSONAL				
Initial Impression				
Rapport				
Level of Sensitivity				
Enthusiasm				
Self Confidence				
Instils Confidence				
Sensitivity				
Appearance – Business Like?				

KNOWLEDGE				
Industry				
Application				
Product/Service Knowledge				
Business Practices				

	YES	?	NO	
Could I be his/her manager?				

Three areas for improvement	1		2		3	

Overall rating defined as progress for   Instructor:..

Ex		Good		– Satis +			Weak		Unsat		Did harm
Outstanding		Significant		Reasonable			Marginal		None		Did harm

CASE STUDY – ROLE-PLAY BRIEF

THE SITUATION

YOUR OBJECTIVES	
1	
2	
3	
4	

THE REPRESENTATIVE'S OBJECTIVES	
1	
2	
3	
4	
5	
6	
7	
8	

OBJECTIONS TO BE RAISED BY YOU	
1	
2	
3	
4	

CALL EVALUATION

At the end of the allotted time, the instructor should elicit from each member of the observing team one good point and one bad point but should take the trouble to look at the objectives that the salesperson had set him/herself and compare them with the actual objectives achieved.

Emphasis during the de-brief should focus upon preparedness, control, use of references and concern about over-committing resources.

In overall terms, the instructor should assess confidentially the following points:

- Would I like to be this person's manager?

- Could I work for this person?

GENERAL

In general terms, the Instructor must use his judgement as to how to play this call depending on the approach of the salesperson who is making the call.

There should be no deliberate provocation although a degree of 'prospect licence' is certainly allowed. Remember that the only person in the scenario who is acting is the Instructor – the salesperson must approach the task as if it were real.

Best Answers

Q.1: C

Q.2: A

Q.3: A

Q.4: E

Q.5: All

Q.6: A

Q.7: All

Q.8: All

Q.9: All

Q.10: B, C, E, G

Q.11: A, B, C, F

Q.12: All

Q.13: A, C, E

Q.14: A, B, C, E, F, G

Q.15: C, D, E

Q.16: A, B, C, D

Q.17: A, C, E, F, G, I,

Q.18: Agree A-F

Q.19: Agree A-G

Q.20: C

Q.21: B, C, D, E, F

Q.22: None

Q.23: A, B, C, D

Q.24: True

Q.25: All

Q.26: Desirable

Q.27: Necessary

Q.28: All

Q.29: A

Q.30: A, B, C, E

Q.31: A, B, C, D, E, F

SCORE

25–31: You are already very aware of the benefits of a talent management programme and capable of implementing one yourself, immediately.

18–24: You appear to be committed to a talent management programme and you should seek assistance in your company to implement it as soon as possible.

15–23: You may not be yet convinced of the benefits but you need to speak to internal/external advisors to get you to see what could be achieved.

Less than 23: Read the book again and really think about the messages contained therein that could help you and your company achieve so much more.

Index

About the Authors

Maggie Cutt

Maggie Cutt is a professional HR Consultant who is currently advising a UK trade association on policies and strategies. She is a Member of the Chartered Institute of Personnel and Development.

Much of her career has been spent in the computing services sector, which included periods with BIS and the Hoskyns Group (now Cap Gemini). She is a professional HR Manager with around 30 years' HR experience. She is an all-round HR generalist with particular expertise in employee relations and is currently operating as an independent HR Consultant.

Tony Davis

Tony Davis is Product Line Director at SkillsEdge Limited, a provider of assessment and training services and Senior Partner with SST International. He had a long career with IBM in both line and staff management positions prior to establishing SST International to provide customized training for the IT industry.

His first book, *Selling Professional Services*, was a guide to assisting people new to selling complex IT systems. His most recent work, in conjunction with Richard Pharro of the APM group, is *The Relationship Manager – the Next Generation of Project Management* published by Gower in 2003.

Neil Flynn

Neil has a distinguished background in software and consultancy-related solutions. He has worked for some major software houses in senior manager/ director positions such as Comshare, Thorn EMI, Computershare, IBM, IOC and SST International. His client experience includes a wide range of industries within the IT sector such as Insurance, Banking and Finance, Telecommunications, Retail, Petroleum and Automotive.

Neil has extensive experience in a very wide variety of both psychometric and knowledge-based assessment processes, being one of the key contributing authors of a number of methods of personnel measurement. In addition to other external responsibilities, Neil is CEO of SkillsEdge Limited.

Peter Mowl

Peter Mowl is Technical Director at SkillsEdge Limited and has been responsible for customer services and support with a number of large UK organizations including ICL. He also had a series of technical consultancy and management appointments culminating in his appointment as Senior Project Manager for a UK building society responsible for the installation of a large ICL network. His last appointment was a Technical Director with Able Hosting Ltd where, joining forces with SST International, Peter became one of the founder directors of SkillsEdge Limited specializing in web-based knowledge assessments for business professionals.

Simon Orme

Simon Orme has worked in the computer and computer services sectors since 1965. He worked for ICL in the UK and Australia and spent three years as System Development Manager with the Ministry of Finance in Fiji.

On his return to the UK he joined Hoskyns as a consultant. He was subsequently Managing Director of Lonsdale Systems and BIS Insurance Systems before rejoining Hoskyns (which later became Cap Gemini) as a Divisional Managing Director in 1983.

He retired from Cap Gemini in 1992 and formed Simon Orme and Associates as Managing Partner. He is Chairman of SkillsEdge Limited and an advisor to and investor in a number of leading computer services companies.